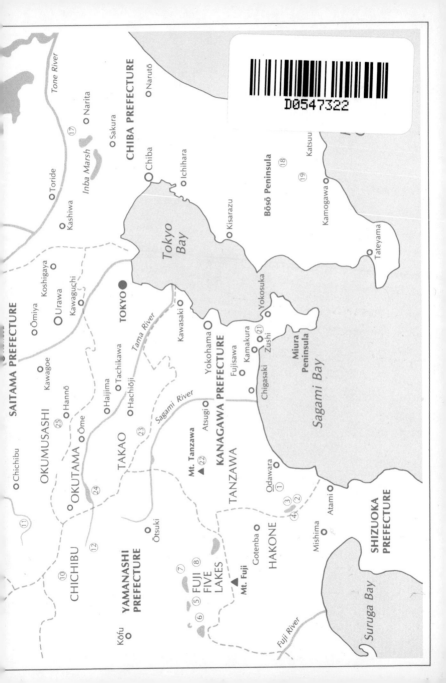

More Day Walks Near Tokyo

More Day Walks Near Tokyo

by Gary D'A. Walters

KODANSHA INTERNATIONAL
Tokyo, New York, London

To all friends of our Earth

Cover illustrations by Tarō Higuchi
Maps by Tadamitsu Ōmori
Endpaper map by Yasunori Yoshida

Distributed in the United States by Kodansha America, Inc., 114 Fifth Avenue, New York, N.Y. 10011, and in the United Kingdom and continental Europe by Kodansha Europe Ltd., Gillingham House, 38-44 Gillingham Street, London SW1V 1HU. Published by Kodansha International Ltd., 17-14 Otowa 1-chome, Bunkyo-ku, Tokyo 112, and Kodansha America, Inc.

92 93 10 9 8 7 6 5 4 3 2 1

Library of Congress Cataloging-in-Publication Data

Walters, Gary D'A.
    More day walks near Tokyo / by Gary D'A.
Walters.—1st ed.
          p.   cm.
    Summary: Outlines twenty-five walking trips at the outer edge of Tokyo, all of which can be completed in a single day and which feature natural and historical sites of interest.
    ISBN 4-7700-1592-5 (Japan)
    1. Walking—Japan—Kantō Region—Guidebooks. 2. Hiking—Japan—Kantō Region—Guidebooks. 3. Kantō Region (Japan)—Guidebooks. [1. Hiking—Japan—Kantō Region—Guides. 2. Kantō Region (Japan)—Guides.] I. Title.
GV199.44.J32K368 1992
915.2'13—dc20   91-45364
                                                        CIP
                                                         AC

CONTENTS

PREFACE

Welcome to the wonderful world of Kantō District walking—the greatest natural cure for jaded Tokyoites living and working in one of the busiest, most densely populated cities in the world! This book will guide you away from the high-rises of Japan's capital and into (and back out of) some of the most attractive countryside you could hope to see—all within a few hours of the metropolis. *Day Walks Near Tokyo*, the companion volume to this publication, offered "towering snow-capped mountains in winter, fast-flowing streams racing through breathtaking ravines in summer, brilliantly colored forests in autumn, an abundance of wildflowers in spring." To these you can now add gushing waterfalls, gentle lakeside trails, paths steeped in history, ancient temples and eerie castle sites, monkeys, deer and other native animals, ice-cool lava caves, volcanic steam vents and soothing hot springs, and of course those wonderful Fuji views!

All the walks in this guide can be completed in a single day, though some of these places are so stunning you will want to stay longer. For that reason, in some instances I have included suggestions for accommodation. The paths described are practicable for anyone of reasonable fitness, although the rugged topography of Japan makes for occasional steep climbs. (Alas, almost everywhere flat in the Kantō District has been built on.)

Thus, walkers with little previous experience should probably begin with the easier trails. Note that the word "walk" rather than "hike" (which sounds too much like hard work to me!) has been used. "Ramble" or "tramp" could just as easily have been applied.

The twenty-five trails described here cover in greater detail the outer areas touched on only lightly in *Day Walks Near Tokyo* (and accordingly do not include many in the inner regions concentrated on in that book), thus making the two volumes complementary. As you might expect, these outer areas generally have considerably more to offer walkers, though naturally the transport charges are a little higher. Included are parts of the beautiful Fuji-Hakone-Izu, Takao, Chichibu-Tama, and Nikkō national parks.

Places of interest encountered along the trail are described, especially temples, shrines, and historical sites, and the wildflowers, birds, and occasional wild animal likely to be seen are indicated. Suitable places to stop for lunch are also suggested. (References such as John Whitney Hall's *Japan From Prehistory To Modern Times* [Charles E. Tuttle, 1987] will give you a good overview of some of the famous names and events of Japanese history referred to in the text.) The description of each walk assumes that the reader is *not* familiar with the Japanese language and provides easy-to-follow instructions, with Japanese signboards reproduced in the text together with their English translations. Readers not familiar with country walking in general are advised to read the introductory sections, and it is recommended that all readers skim through at least the "Getting There" section before commencing their journey, so that they can decide on the optimum departure time.

Finally, a few words on walking etiquette: *Do* remember to take away your meal leftovers so that others can also enjoy the forests in their pristine state, and *don't* forget to respect common-sense rules regarding the preservation of flora and fauna.

Also, it is customary to greet other walkers with a polite *Konnichiwa!* (Good day!).

GARY D'A. WALTERS

Acknowledgments

In any project of this kind, there are always numerous people whose assistance with walk suggestions, translations, checking names, and the like has been important. Kotaro Nitta, Jonathan Holliman, Aiko Nakajima, Mutsumi Teramura and, in particular, Kazuyo Masuda, Keiko Ishikawa, and Suzanne Walters-Quan are just some of those who made essential contributions. Thanks also to Jules Young and Michiko Uchiyama, the editors, and to Tadamitsu Ōmori, who drew the maps. To these people and many others, I extend my deepest gratitude.

INTRODUCTION

Using This Guide

This guide is divided into five sections focusing on the areas of Hakone, the Fuji Five Lakes, Chichibu (including Oku-chichibu), Nikkō, and Ibaraki-Chiba (which also covers the Bōsō Peninsula), with a brief introduction for each section followed by four walks. A further five walks in closer areas (Tanzawa, Miura Peninsula, Takao, Okutama, and Oku-musashi) are also included, making a total of twenty-five walks. The locations of all the walks are indicated by their number on the map printed on the endpapers.

Beside the title of each walk, the letter "E" (standing for easy), "M" (for moderate), or "D" (for relatively difficult) appears. These ratings are based on the length of the walk as well as the steepness of the path, and represent a simple measure of the degree of difficulty to assist the reader in choosing a walk. Within each section, the walks are presented in order of increasing difficulty. The trails have to some degree been chosen so that bus rides occur at the start rather than the end of the walk (to avoid missing the last bus) and, where possible, so that you walk from a higher elevation to a lower one. An appendix at the back of the guide contains additional classifications of suggested walks according to the season, and a list of five recommended walks for the visitor with limited time.

At the beginning of each walk, information is presented under four headings. The first gives a brief outline of the course, occasionally with alternative routes indicated. The second specifies the reference maps that are useful. (Though these are certainly not essential, they do give a good perspective of your overall location and are discussed later in this Introduction.) The third heading gives the approximate walking time. Note that walking times are only intended as a rough guide for two to four "average" walkers, and don't include rest stops, lunch, sightseeing, and so on. Thus, a trail rated "E" but with several attractions could easily become a relaxing, all-day affair. Naturally, actual times depend on the individual's walking pace and the size of the group, and considerable time should be allowed for breaks. The fourth and final heading lists features of interest encountered on the way.

Then follows an introductory section, titled "Getting There," that describes the main public transport options for reaching the beginning of the path, including the exact cost at the time of writing. Of course, prices and fares rise with time, but around Tokyo fare increases are usually infrequent, and when they do occur, they are relatively small. These prices can therefore be considered a fairly reliable guide for the next few years at least. (In fact, a check of ticket prices listed in *Day Walks Near Tokyo* revealed that on average they had risen by less than 5 percent after several years.) Some walkers' fares will differ if you are boarding from a station other than the one suggested. In this case, it is worth remembering that you can always purchase the minimum price ticket and pay the balance to the conductor on the train or to the ticket collector (in some cases at the Fare Adjustment Window) at your destination or a transfer point.

Timetables for trains and buses are complicated and, especially for the latter, sometimes subject to seasonal change. Thus, the times listed cannot be considered infallible. For this reason, I have provided an indication of the frequency of early morning trains (where expedient or possible), and some alternatives to infrequent buses.

As a general compromise to the problem that walkers will set out from different areas of Tokyo, I have usually listed as the starting points either major JR (Japan Railways) Yamanote Line (山手線) stations or their nearby private line counterparts. Note that the platform numbers mentioned in this section refer only to platforms in that part of the station belonging to the particular line. (Most major stations have several different lines, each with the same platform numbers).

If the return transport is significantly different from that used for the start of the trail, details are given at the end of the walk description.

For Yokohama residents, the following lines may be used as convenient shortcuts to the start of the walks or to the lines listed in the "Getting There" sections:

To Fuji Five Lakes: JR Yokohama Line (横浜線) to the Chūō Main Line's Hachiōji (八王子) Station.

To Hakone: JR Tōkaidō Line (東海道線) to Odawara (小田原) Station.

To Tanzawa: JR Tōkaidō Line to Fujisawa (藤沢) Station, then Odakyū Enoshima Line (小田急 江ノ島線) to the Odakyū Line's Sagami-Ōno (相模大野) Station.

To Takao: JR Yokohama Line to Hachiōji Station, then JR Chūō Line (中央線) to the Keiō Line's Takao (高尾) Station.

To Okutama: JR Yokohama and Hachikō (八高線) lines to the JR Ōme Line's Haijima (拝島) Station.

To Okumusashi: JR Yokohama and Hachikō lines to the Tōbu Tōjō Ogose Line's Ogose (越生) Station.

To Chichibu: JR Yokohama and Hachikō lines to the Chichibu Railway's Yorii (寄居) Station, and (for Oku-chichibu [奥秩父]) JR Yokohama Line to the Chūō Line's Hachiōji Station.

The description of each walk that follows the "Getting

There" section is divided into two or three linking route segments (between stations, bus stops, and landmarks), each with its own total walking time indicated. The signposts you encounter as you walk present something of a problem in as much as the Japanese may be written from left to right, from top to bottom, or, occasionally, from right to left. In the first two cases, I have presented the Japanese (usually in parentheses after the English translation and/or romanized Japanese) in the order from left to right, but in the third case I have retained the right to left order, hopefully to avoid confusing readers with little knowledge of Japanese, since this is how they will see it. General directions are also mostly presented with their translations or romanized Japanese followed by the Japanese characters in parentheses. Note that Japanese characters can often be written in several ways, so it is possible to see partly or even totally different signs for the same destination. The English-language terms "path," "trail," and "track" have been used synonymously.

Within the linking walk segments, times are given between various landmarks or, if only a destination landmark is mentioned, between the previous place to which a time was given and this new landmark. The times provided for sloping paths are only pertinent to the direction of travel that is described, whether uphill or downhill. Snow-covered or muddy ground will increase these times considerably. Information regarding alternative (including shortened) routes and the directions of other paths from intersections is provided where useful or of interest. Since landmarks change with time—roads and housing estates are constructed, signs disappear or become illegible, and sometimes new boards are added—try to use a little common sense if the written description no longer seems to match the actual terrain.

Each walk is accompanied by a detailed sketch map that shows many of the minor trails branching off; the sketch map and the description are intended to be read in conjunction with each other. Because some parts of the indicated route may be exaggerated in order to show certain features more clearly, the scale on the sketch map should only be regarded as an indication of the distances involved and not as an accurate measure. In some cases, the scale does not permit all details to be illustrated, and thus it is essential to read the descriptive text. The symbols used in the sketch maps are:

- - - - - - The Route of the Walk
————— Other Walking Track
▬▬▬▬ Road
▬▬ ▬ ▬ JR Railway Line
+++++ Other Railway Line
◯——— Bus Stop
卍 Temple
卅 Shrine
𖠿 Other Building (mountain hut, inn, etc.)
▲ Mountain/Peak
✕ Trail Blocked Off or Dead End
⟐ Good Views

The accommodation suggestions listed for some of the more distant walks consist mostly of "pensions" (small modern lodging houses with private rooms, communal sitting and dining rooms, often serving Western-style meals) or *minshuku* (cheaper, Japanese-style accommodation) that I have stayed at myself and found to be satisfactory, and sometimes delightful. Many alternatives exist that are equally pleasant or even better, so don't be afraid to follow your own judgment when choosing a place to stay. (Incidentally, a number of pensions or *minshuku* that request bookings by telephone to be made in Japanese often have staff or a family member who can speak a little English, so don't be discouraged if you are not fluent in Japanese.)

Preparing for Walks

Although one-day walks do not require a great deal of preparation, a few things can make them more enjoyable. These include obtaining a suitable pack, clothing, and footwear; taking sufficient food and drink; and adequate planning beforehand with respect to maps and travel and walking times to ensure that the walk can be completed within a day. These aspects are covered below.

One other hint for weekend walkers: if you can walk on a Saturday rather than a Sunday (although in a few cases this will mean some buses are not running), you will find the trails considerably less crowded.

PACKS

A good pack is essential to hold all the items you need and to free your hands for other purposes, such as reading maps and guides, photography, birdwatching, as well as maintaining balance. Probably the best kind of pack is a larger version of the waterproof, frameless day-packs commonly used by Japanese children when they go on excursions. It should feel comfortable when packed.

CLOTHING

The main requirement is to dress suitably for the season, taking into account that temperatures can drop fairly rapidly, especially near the summit of a windswept mountain, whereas, equally importantly, exertion results in the body heating up. It is, therefore, better to dress in layers that can be easily removed or added to. A warm jacket and gloves are absolutely essential in winter, and a light waterproof jacket or, at the very least, a sweater is a good idea at any time of the year. Jackets with a pocket large enough to hold a map or guidebook are best, since repeatedly reaching into a pack for these can be annoying. Winter and summer hats are also recommended to reduce heat loss and sunburn, respectively. If you intend to stop at a hot spring, don't forget to bring a small towel.

FOOTWEAR

Although many day walkers can be seen wearing running shoes or the like, these can be inadequate for tougher walks. On the other hand, expensive hiking boots are not worth purchasing unless you also intend to use them for longer, more arduous hikes. The best compromise is a pair of sturdy walking shoes or ankle-high hiking boots (without lace-up gaiters) that provide good support on inclines. Choose good-quality leather or nylon-mesh boots that allow your feet to "breathe." As with all shoes, walking boots should be worn in before a long walk, and should be cleaned afterwards to prevent deterioration.

FOOD AND DRINK

A hearty breakfast is a good prelude to a day's walk—it will have plenty of time to settle on the train before you reach the start of the trail. Although food eaten during a walk is a matter of personal taste, it should be nourishing—Japanese *bentō* (boxed lunches) and *onigiri* (rice balls) sold at or near railway stations make convenient lunches—and sufficient, since food is rarely available along the route. Some walkers feel that a series of light snacks is better than one large meal. In any case, something to provide a little energy late in the afternoon comes in handy.

As for drinks, the "sports" formulas are very good in summer, whereas hot drinks go a long way toward reviving flagging spirits in winter. In addition to these, a container (preferably of the light, collapsible type) of drinking water should be carried. Again, canned drinks and water are often not available along the route, and should be obtained from railway stations or near the start of the walk.

MAPS AND TIME PLANNING

The sketch maps that accompany each walk should suffice, so the maps mentioned under the heading "Reference map" are not strictly required. However, they are useful in determining the route if some change in the landscape has occurred, as well as for the reasons given below.

In the absence of English-language material, the most suitable walking maps in Japan are the Japanese-language Nitchi series of *Tozan haikingu* (ニッチ 登山 ハイキングシリーズ, "Mountain Climbing and Hiking") and Shōbunsha's *Yama to kōgen* (昭文社 山と高原地図, "Mountains and Highlands"). The original series of both have been replaced with new ones containing nearly identical maps, at a price of ¥700. The relevant numbers of the new and old maps for both series are listed at the beginning of each walk description.

Also useful are the large-scale (1:25,000) Geographical Survey Institute (国土地理院) sheet maps, which cost ¥270. Although the larger scale of these maps makes them helpful for some walks, the Nitchi and Shōbunsha series have the advantage of better displaying the more recognized walking trails and giving details of bus connections to the paths. All of these publications are available from major bookstores.

The easiest method of finding your way around these maps is to use the map's main landmark index, or, if there is none, to locate the appropriate railway line and then let your eye follow this to the station mentioned. From there, you should be able to find a key element of the walking course, such as a major mountain or a road leading to the bus stop (in the case of the Nitchi and Shōbunsha maps, often marked in red in a small box and approximately identifiable by the travel time given) at the start of the walk.

When using a map and compass, the map should be laid horizontal and then rotated to align its north marker with the compass needle. Subsequently, landmarks can be identified with respect to your own position from the direction indicated by the map.

Although the task of time planning, that is, determining a route whose times (including travel) are realistic for a single day, has already been undertaken for the walks in this guide, it is usually necessary to start out early, preferably between 6:00 and 7:00 A.M., depending on your starting point, to allow for the possibility of poor train and bus connections and other delays. Keeping an eye on the time while walking is important, because mountain paths become dangerous as darkness falls (which happens quite early in winter) and bus services usually cease operating at about 6:00 or 7:00 P.M., or even earlier. Six hours of walking is considered a comfortable limit for most people.

Transportation

Readers familiar with at least basic Japanese will have little trouble using Japanese-language *jikokuhyō*, the comprehensive timetable books put out by JTB (Japan Travel Bureau) and JR (Japan Railways). The larger versions cost about ¥850 and list the times of most trains, many buses, and some other means of transport. To locate the correct page, look at the appropriate map at the start of the book, find the particular train or bus route, and then turn to the page indicated for the schedules. Most bookstores stock *jikokuhyō*.

For many hiking areas near Tokyo, passes are available that permit travel to and from, as well as within, the area—*jiyūkippu* (freedom tickets) are usually only valid for trains, while *furiipasu* (free passes) frequently also include use of buses and cable cars for sightseeing. Most of these are only worthwhile if you spend a few days in the area and move around a lot. The most useful of these are suggested where relevant.

The total cost of transport (train and, if applicable, bus) for the walks described in this guide ranges from ¥880 to ¥6,900, with ¥3,500 as the average.

Note that (1) due to probable road congestion, weekend highway buses cannot be recommended as a means of getting to the start of a trail, although they might be satisfactory for returning; and (2) although several alternatives often exist (only the best and most straightforward of which are listed here) for catching trains and, in particular, the subsequent buses, in order to get a seat for a long journey it is wise to board at the terminus of the bus going to the start of the trail and at the terminus of the train returning to Tokyo, and the suggestions in this guide are usually based on this principle.

TRAINS

The destination, type, and departure time of trains (in addition to being announced in Japanese) are often displayed on an overhead sign just inside the ticket barrier, particularly in the larger terminus stations of Tokyo. This sign will also usually list the next few trains and the platforms they leave from. Otherwise, train information can be obtained from the sign or the timetable near or on the appropriate platform. A final check of the destination may be made by looking at the front (or the side) of the train itself. The type of train (express, limited express, etc.) is sometimes displayed on the front of the train, at other times on the side.

The timetables themselves are rather more complex affairs, with different symbols used to mark destinations and train types. Note that 平日 (often in blue) refers to Monday to Saturday, while 休日 (red) is for Sundays and public holidays.

For some walks, the possibility of catching faster trains with a surcharge is discussed. The basic ticket is known as a *jōshaken* (passenger ticket) and the supplementary fare as a *tokkyūken* (limited express ticket). Purchasing a *tokkyūken* does not necessarily entitle you to a reserved seat (known as a *shiteiseki*), which may cost a little more. On trains with reserved seats, however, there are usually also carriages with unreserved seating.

BUSES

Unlike Tokyo city buses, which you usually board at the front, paying a fixed fare as you get on, longer-distance country buses have their entrance at the rear or middle, and the fare, which depends on the distance traveled, is paid when you get off (at the front). Except when boarding at the terminus (or in the first sector of the route), you should take a ticket from the machine next to the steps as you board the bus. The number on this ticket is later used to determine your fare from the illuminated board visible at the front of the bus near the driver. Most buses referred to in this guide are of this variable-fare type.

Note that (1) different timetables often apply for weekdays/Saturdays and Sundays/public holidays, as with trains; (2) bus journey times are dependent on prevailing traffic conditions, which vary especially in Nikkō and Hakone; and (3) the bus terminuses referred to in the "Getting There" section as being the point to alight may be merely vacant areas of land rather than any structure.

For a small group of walkers, if the bus is too infrequent or not running, consider taking a taxi—it may well be just as cheap on a per-person basis as the bus fare. Check the approximate cost with the taxi driver first.

Safety and Comfort

Since most of the routes in this guide are not too far away from at least a farmhouse, should you lose your way there is little cause for worry if you use your common sense. Care is definitely needed on paths up or down steep slopes and across ridges with adjacent sheer drops. Occasionally in summer, wasps and basking snakes can be a hazard. (Although many publications claim that on Japan's main island of Honshū, only one species of snake, the *mamushi* (Halys viper), is venomous, I have been told that there is at least one other kind, so caution is warranted.) The potential dangers and discomforts of walks can be minimized by taking the following steps:

1. Check the weather forecast before leaving home. If rain is likely, postpone the walk. Slippery slopes in areas such as Tanzawa and Okutama can be treacherous. Avoid walking in excessively hot conditions or in remote regions with heavy snow cover.

2. Let someone know where you are going and, of course, inform them on your return.

3. Carry a map and compass. If you lose your way, these may be of help in providing some idea of your location from reference map contours and surrounding landmarks.

4. Take sufficient food and drink in case the walk lasts longer than expected. Waterproof matches for lighting fires and a small flashlight (which is also useful for exploring caves) are sensible emergency items to carry.

5. On some walks, particularly in summer, insect spray will be well worth taking.

6. Don't walk alone. Three adults is usually considered the minimum safe number. Stay together and make sure all members of the group have a copy of the route.

7. Stop frequently for rests, and travel at a pace comfortable for the slowest member of the group. It is also wise to pace yourself by not walking too fast too early, and by slowing down on steep ascents.

Emergency Japanese

Generally, you will find that not only are Japanese people friendly and helpful but also many of them, particularly city people (who are often fellow walkers), can speak a little English. However, should you have difficulty in making yourself understood, the following basic words and phrases will assist you in obtaining directions, identifying landmarks, and communicating in case of emergency. (Using the Japanese name for a landmark when enquiring will greatly facilitate this process.) For these words and phrases, the Hepburn system, in which so-called long "o" and "u" vowels are denoted by a bar above the vowel, has been used. (The vowel sounds are approximately: "a" as in "father," "e" as in "egg," "i" as in "pin," "o" as in "cough," and "u" as in "put.")

Mt. . . .   . . . *yama* or   . . . *san (zan)* 山

... Peak   ... *mine* 峰 or 嶺
... Hill (Peak)   ... *tsuka* (*zuka*) 塚
... Pass   ... *tōge* 峠
Lake ...   ... *ko* 湖
... River   ... *kawa* (*gawa*) 川
Cape ...   ... *saki* (*zaki*) 崎
... Temple   ... *tera* (*dera*) or   ... *ji* 寺
... Shrine   ... *jinja* 神社
station *eki* 駅
bus stop *basu tei* バス停
direction *hōmen* 方面
left *hidari* 左
right *migi* 右
straight on *massugu* まっすぐ
toilet *otearai* 御手洗い or お手洗い
thank you *arigatō* ありがとう

Does this train/bus go to . . . ?
Kono densha/basu wa . . . e ikimasu ka?
この電車/バスは……へ行きますか.
Please tell me when we reach . . .
. . . *ni tsuitara oshiete kudasai.*
…に着いたら教えて下さい.
Is this the way to . . . ?
Kochira wa . . . hōmen desu ka?
こちらは…方面ですか.
I am/My friend is sick/injured. Please help me.
Watashi/Tomodachi wa byoki desu/kega shimashita. Tasukete kudasai.
私/友達は病気です/ケガしました. 助けて下さい.

Birdwatching and Wildflower Field Guides

Birdwatchers need look no further than the excellent *A Field Guide to the Birds of Japan*, by the Wild Bird Society of Japan (published by the Wild Bird Society of Japan in cooperation with Kodansha International Ltd., 1986). *A Birdwatcher's Guide to Japan*, by Mark Brazil (published by Kodansha International Ltd. in cooperation with the Wild Bird Society of Japan, 1987) is also a useful book.

Wildflower enthusiasts, would-be dendrologists, and edible berry and plant gourmets, however, are not so well catered for, the only English-language publication of which I am aware being incomplete and not particularly pertinent. There does exist, though, a wealth of Japanese-language material, including field guides according to season, region, and type of plant. The plant names in these are usually presented in *kana* (the Japanese phonetic scripts), which require a knowledge of only one hundred or so letters, rather than the thousands of *kanji* (Chinese characters) commonly used in Japanese. The flowers named in this book were for the most part identified using the comprehensive, well-illustrated references *Nihon no yasō* (日本の野草) (Wildflowers of Japan; Yama-kei, 1983) and *Nihon no jumoku* (日本の樹木) (Woody Plants of Japan; Yama-kei, 1985).

Japanese-language publications on fungi, mushrooms, insects, animals (and even their tracks), and a host of related subjects are also readily available.

Further Walking

Unfortunately, there is virtually no other detailed English-language publication devoted to hiking near Tokyo except the companion to this guide, *Day Walks Near Tokyo* (Kodansha International, 1988). However, if some degree of confidence can be developed with the hiking maps mentioned, the possibilities are endless. A quick glance at some of these maps will show the many red lines representing walking trails, as well as access to the walks by bus and train.

The walks in this guide are of the one-day kind, but if you have time two-day walks are equally feasible, although more preparation and planning are required. The Izu Peninsula and Ōze are relatively close areas not described here that you might like to try. For such walks, it is possible to stay overnight in mountain cabins, the locations of which are also marked on some walking maps. Walkers wishing to go on longer sojourns are fortunate in that a good English-language guide, Paul Hunt's *Hiking in Japan* (Kodansha International, 1988), is available.

Another possibility is to join a walking club or an organization that features walking as one of its activities. Such groups in Tokyo include Friends of the Earth, tel. (03) 3770-5387, and the International Adventure Club, tel. (03) 3333-0419 or (03) 3327-2905, which include both Japanese and foreign members. Even if you don't wish to walk regularly with a number of people, these group walks can open up interesting new directions to you.

Happy walking!

HAKONE

This popular summer retreat consists of a group of reasonably high forested peaks wedged between the Izu Peninsula and Mt. Fuji and centering around the once-active volcano Mt. Hakone. The area offers walkers nature's best in the form of forest, fast-flowing rivers, waterfalls, hot springs, and the picturesque Lake Ashi, as well as a slice of absorbing history. Located in Kanagawa Prefecture, Hakone also boasts a number of endemic species of flora. All of the trails described here are within the Fuji-Hakone-Izu National Park, which lies to the southwest of Tokyo. The Odakyū Line from Shinjuku and the Hakone Tozan Line out of Odawara/Hakone-Yumoto, plus numerous local buses, provide good access to all sections of the region.

1. OLD YUSAKA ROAD ———————————— E

Course: Kowaki-dani Station → Chisuji Waterfall → Mt. Sengen → Hakone-Yumoto Station

Alternative course: Miya-no-shita Station → Mt. Sengen → Mt. Taka-no-su → Hiryū Falls → Hatajuku (by bus) → Hakone-Yumoto Station

Reference map: Nitchi Map No. 26 (Hakone, 箱根), Old Series No. 7; or Shōbunsha Map No. 19 (Hakone).

Walking time: About 2 hours 10 minutes.

Points of interest: Native forest and spring and summer wild-flowers, numerous birds, the old (Yusaka) road to Kamakura, Chisu-ji Waterfall, and the site of Yusaka Castle. The alternative course passes the site of Taka-no-su Castle and spectacular Hiryū Falls.

GETTING THERE

From Shinjuku Station, take an Odakyū Line (小田急線) express (*kyūkō*, 急行) (Platform 4 or 5) or the faster limited express (*tokkyū*, 特急), called the "Romance Car" (Platform 2 or 3, ¥800 surcharge), to Hakone-Yumoto (箱根湯本) Station, and then transfer to the Hakone Tozan Railway (箱根登山鉄道) and ride to Kowaki-dani (小涌谷) Station. However, since relatively few trains go all the way to

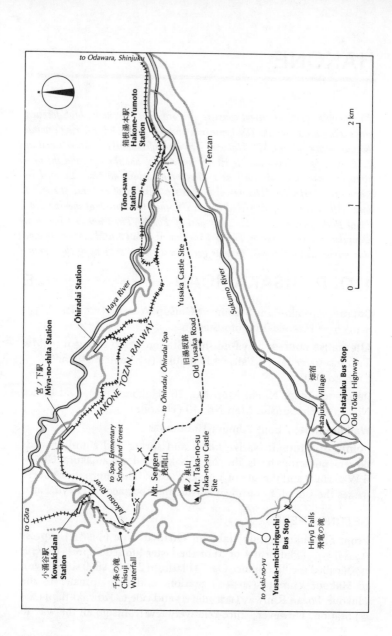

Hakone-Yumoto, it may be necessary to catch an express to Odawara (小田原), where you can also transfer to the Hakone Tozan Railway.

It is simplest to purchase a ticket for the journey to Odawara (¥750), and then pay the balance of ¥470 on the train or at your destination for the last leg on the Hakone Tozan Railway. The journey to Odawara takes 1 hour 25–40 minutes (to Hakone-Yumoto requires a further 10 minutes).

As the Odakyū Line branches at Sagami-Ōno (相模大野) Station, make sure that you are on a train bound for Odawara or Hakone-Yumoto, and *not* Enoshima (江ノ島). Also, some trains divide at Sagami-Ōno, with the front and rear having different destinations, so be sure to board one of the front carriages.

At Odawara, to transfer to the Hakone Tozan Railway, simply go along the platform toward the front of the train until you reach the section (known as Platforms 11 and 12) from where this little two-car train resembling a municipal tram departs. To change at Hakone-Yumoto, walk forward and around to adjacent Platform 4. The extremely scenic 42–49-minute journey (31–36 minutes from Hakone-Yumoto) up the Haya River valley to Kowaki-dani involves reversing direction at several switchbacks. In summer, the route is lined with the colorful flowers of various kinds of *ajisai* (hydrangea), and the train passes above the old spa towns of Tōno-sawa and Miya-no-shita.

From Kowaki-dani Station to Mt. Sengen (45 minutes)

Leaving Kowaki-dani (Kowaki Valley) Station, follow the vehicle road the short distance up to the main road, where there is a map-board. Cross the main road and walk up the bitumen road on the other side.

Veer left along the small lane you meet after about 5 minutes. A sign here indicates that this is the direction of Chisuji Waterfall (*Chisuji-no-taki*, 千条の滝). This flat lane passes a stand of bamboo and goes through native forest before you come to a car barrier and a sign pointing in the direction of Chisuji Waterfall and Mt. Sengen (*Sengen-yama*) (千条ノ滝 浅間山). A little farther (8 minutes or so after turning off the bitumen road), you should see Chisuji Waterfall on your right, opposite picnic tables.

Chisuji Waterfall on the way to Mt. Sengen.

Although this waterfall is small, it is unusual both in its position and arrangement: it lies outside the pretty Jakotsu River (*Jakotsugawa*), which is some 20 meters away, and the water flows attractively down a sheer wide wall.

The trail continues across the nearby bridge, toward Mt. Sengen and Mt. Taka-no-su (*Taka-no-su-yama*) (浅間山 鷹ノ巣山). Bear right on the other side, ignoring the small path to the left that follows the river downstream. Within a minute, the trail splits into two. To the right runs a lower track that parallels the river in the direction of Mt. Taka-no-su and Ashi-no-yu (鷹ノ巣山 芦之湯), passing through forest with *aburachan* (*Parabenzoin praecox*) and *kuromoji* (lindera or spicebush) trees. The path to the left climbs toward Mt. Sengen (浅間山). Take the latter, uphill path.

This rocky trail, crisscrossed by the roots of the native forest, becomes quite steep. Avoid the path leading to a dead-end that you find to the right after a few minutes. In places the path forks, usually only to reunite a short distance later, except for one track that leads to a small shrine a short distance away. Dwarf bamboo grows on the trail sides, and later the vegetation changes to *sugi* (cedar) plantations and then bamboo.

Among the many avian residents and visitors in the surrounding woods are *akagera* (great spotted woodpecker), *kogera* (Japanese pygmy woodpecker), *aogera* (Japanese green woodpecker), *kakesu* (jay), *uguisu* (bush warbler), *yabusame* (short-tailed bush warbler), *ikaru* (Japanese grosbeak), *higara* (coal tit), *yamagara* (varied tit), *shijūkara* (great tit), *misosazai* (winter wren), *kibitaki* (narcissus flycatcher), *kiji* (common pheasant), and *hashibutogarasu* (jungle crow).

After approximately 25 minutes, turn to the right toward Mt. Sengen. (Straight ahead is the path to Miya-no-shita [宮ノ下], while the overgrown track to the left leads to a spa, a primary school, and a forest [温泉小学校植林地入口].) From here, the going is a little easier through relatively flat forest containing *aoki* (laurel) trees, and in less than 5 minutes you will arrive at another intersection, where there is a picnic table and benches. In front of you is a wide trail—the old Yusaka Road (*Yusaka-michi*, once a major thoroughfare to Kamakura in the time of the Kamakura shogunate (1185–1333).

A sign here points to Mt. Taka-no-su, Ashi-no-yu, and Hata-juku (鷹ノ巣山 芦ノ湯 畑宿) to the right. This route would make an interesting diversion or even part of a completely new walk (see the alternative course described in detail at the end of this walk), as Mt. Taka-no-su (about 20 minutes away) was the site of a minor castle used by Toyotomi Hideyoshi's troops in his 1590 march on the Go-Hōjō stronghold of Odawara Castle. Beyond is Yusaka-michi-iriguchi (湯坂路入口) Bus Stop, and, farther, the spectacular Hiryū Falls (飛竜の滝) and Hatajuku (畑宿) Bus Stop.

However, the walk described here follows the old Yusaka Road to the east, labeled "Ōhiradai and Yumoto" (大平台 湯本), so veer left along the wide ridge path to Mt. Sengen (804 meters high), less than a minute away. The location itself and the table and benches make this a good place to stop for lunch. The nearby signboard explains that the name Mt. Sengen (*Sengen-yama*) was adopted in the Edo period (1603–1868) and comes from the Sengen religion associated with Mt. Fuji and Sengen Shrine located on the side of the mountain. Previously, the mountain had been called Shimo-taka-no-su (Lower Taka-no-su).

From Mt. Sengen to Hakone-Yumoto Station (1 hour 25 minutes)

Ignoring the path leading to a dead end (行き止り) to the left, proceed straight ahead down the main trail. About 7 minutes later, you will reach a junction with a path to the left to Ōhiradai (大平台), which has a station on the Hakone Tozan Railway. This direction is also signposted for the Ōhiradai Spa area (大平台温泉郷入口), whose waters could make a pleasant end to a ramble. However, to complete the walk described here, continue straight on down the wide path.

There are many wildflowers along the edges of the Yusaka Road. Late spring/early summer flowers include small yellow *nigana* (*Ixeris dentata*) and *ohebiichigo* (*Potentilla kleiniana*), white-and-gold *harujion* (skevish or fleabane), and purple *noazami* (thistle). Among the summer blooms is the ubiquitous white *dokudami* (*Houttuynia cordata*), which is boiled to make a traditional medicine. Flowering trees include *yamabōshi* (dogwood, large white star-shaped flowers), *utsugi* (white deutzia), and *mizuki* (another kind of dogwood, small white blossoms).

Avoid the small path to the left near the electricity pylon encountered after 8–10 minutes. The main path continues down a forested spur, with considerable numbers of maple, beech, and cherry trees. Some 20–25 minutes later, the trail veers away from the cleared ridge and narrows as it passes through dense bamboo, then zigzags through plantations. After descending many log-and-earth steps, the path re-enters native forest and has a number of sections of stone paving in the style of the original Yusaka Road, although most of this is probably recent.

After 20–25 minutes, you should reach the site of Yusaka Castle. Large boulders lie on either side of the castle site. According to the information board here, the castle was built by Ōmori during the Muromachi period (1333–1573), and it controlled the area from Mikuriya (near Gotemba) to West Sagami. In 1495, Ōmori was killed by Ise Sōzui (perhaps better known as Hōjō Sōun, after whom a nearby temple is named), one of the Go-Hōjō clan who took control of the Mt. Hakone region. Following discord between the Go-Hōjō and Hideyoshi in the late Tenshō era (1573–92), a number of castles, including Yusaka, were constructed or improved to protect Odawara in anticipation of a confrontation. The exact scale of the castle remains uncertain, although the extant earthworks provide some guide.

From the castle, the trail descends steeply through native forest, which is home to squirrels. In about 20 minutes, just past some houses, you will arrive at the main road running through Yumoto Town, where there are many *onsen* (hot spring spa) establishments. Some of these accept customers for a few hours in the daytime. Tenzan (天山), which is about 15 minutes up the Sukumo River valley, is popular with many hikers.

Cross the road, turn right, and follow the main road over the river down to Hakone-Yumoto Station (箱根湯本駅), which is on your left, about 6 minutes away.

At Hakone-Yumoto Station, catch an Odakyū Line express back to Shinjuku (about 1 hour 55 minutes, ¥990). If you enjoyed this area and would like to return and do a different walk, you can start from Miya-no-shita Station and follow the Yusaka Road to a stunning waterfall (see the "Alternative course" below, which is also shown on the map for this walk).

Alternative course: Miya-no-shita to Hatajuku (2 hours 10 minutes)

Take the Hakone Tozan Railway to Miya-no-shita (宮ノ下) Station, one stop before Kowaki-dani (balance of fare, ¥440). Leaving the station by its only exit, turn left down the small road and walk the few meters to where an initially paved path veers off to the left. Follow this pleasant track, which is signposted for Mt. Sengen and Sengen Park (浅間山 浅間公園) and whose sides are adorned in summer with hydrangea, pink *hotarubukuro* (bellflower), white *yukinoshita* (strawberry geranium), and other flowers. The path runs approximately parallel with the railway line and passes some houses and a rest shelter.

At the intersection reached after about 7 minutes, bear hard left, cross the railway line, and continue uphill, following signs for Mt. Sengen (浅間山). *Himeshara* (*Stewartia monodelpha*) and *keyaki* (zelkova) trees flourish in this forest. You should reach the junction near Mt. Sengen (described in the main walk) after about 50 minutes. There, take the wide path to the right, which is the continuation of the old Yusaka Road (*Yusaka-michi*), toward Mt. Taka-no-su, Ashi-no-yu, and Hatajuku (鷹ノ巣山 芦ノ湯 畑宿).

In late spring/early summer, this trail has many butterflies and wildflowers, including delicate white *futarishizuka* (*Chloranthus ser-*

ratus) and small purple *nawashiroichigo* (a low-growing, edible raspberry that bears blood-red fruit in summer), and in summer small white roses. Mt. Taka-no-su (literally, "Mt. Eagle's Nest") is about 20 minutes away, at the top of a steep slope that still has some old paving. On the summit, a signboard gives some information on the mountain's Taka-no-su Castle.

Little is known of this beautifully situated castle, though it is thought to be one of those originally constructed by the Go-Hōjō clan. It is also believed that Ieyasu and Hideyoshi's troops occupied the fortress during the 1590 campaign to take Odawara. On a misty day you can almost hear the cries of battle and the clang of sword on sword around this old site.

The rocky trail down the other side has some superb views before it merges with a country lane along which are a few magnificent *sanshōbara* (wild rose) trees. These produce beautiful pink-and-gold flowers in June. In about 10 minutes, you should reach a junction with a path coming in from the left. Only 50 meters straight ahead is the main road, with Yusaka-michi-iriguchi (湯坂路入口) Bus Stop a minute or two to the left along the road (at the time of writing, buses were running to Odawara until at least 7:00 P.M.). However, turn left down the wide path, which boasts attractive natural canopies. This is signposted for Hatajuku (畑宿) and Hiryū Falls (*Hiryū-no-taki*, 飛竜の滝), and descends steeply down log-and-earth steps in bamboo forest. Follow the signs for Hatajuku, and in 15–20 minutes you will reach a fork with a path to the right to the falls and a path to the left to Hatajuku. The noise of the waterfall should be audible, especially during the rainy season when the stream is swollen. Take the path to the right across a bridge and walk for 100 meters or so to where this awesome sight (*hiryū* means "flying dragon") is best viewed. Note that a nearby sign warns *against* drinking the water.

Afterwards, return to the fork and take the path down toward Hatajuku. Follow similar signs for Hatajuku—the walk will require about 25 minutes. Turn left at the main road and go downhill for about 100 meters to Hatajuku Bus Stop in Hatajuku, a village known for woodcraft. The old Tōkai Highway (*Tōkai-dō*) also passes through Hatajuku (see Walk No. 2). The last bus for Hakone-Yumoto Station leaves Hatajuku at 8:30 P.M. (¥320).

2. OLD TŌKAI HIGHWAY ──────── E

Course: Odawara Station (by bus) → Moto-hakone-chūō Bus Stop → Amazake-jaya → Hatajuku → Sukumogawa (by bus) → Hakone-Yumoto Station

Reference map: Nitchi Map No. 26 (Hakone, 箱根), Old Series No. 7; or Shōbunsha Map No. 19 (Hakone).

Walking time: About 2 hours 25 minutes.

Points of interest: The old stone-paved Tōkai Highway (*Tōkai-dō*) running through native forest, various historic sites, including the old barrier gate site, and views of Lake Ashi (an alternative beginning to the trail).

Note: Part of this trail runs alongside a highway, and thus it is best walked on days other than Sundays or public holidays, when there tends to be more traffic.

GETTING THERE

From Shinjuku Station, take an Odakyū Line (小田急線) express (*kyūkō*, 急行) (Platform 4 or 5) to Odawara (小田原) Station. As the Odakyū Line branches at Sagami-Ōno (相模大野) Station, make sure you are on a train bound for Odawara or Hakone-Yumoto (箱根湯本), and *not* Enoshima (江ノ島). Also, some trains divide at Sagami-Ōno, with the front and rear having different destinations, so be sure to board one of the front carriages. The trip takes 1 hour 25–40 minutes and costs ¥750.

A slightly faster (1 hour 10–15 minutes) and much more comfortable means of reaching Odawara is the limited express (*tokkyū*, 特急) called the "Romance Car," from Platform 2 or 3 on the same line. Note, however, that this train is less frequent, often requires booking in advance, and has a ¥800 surcharge.

At Odawara Station, pass through the central Odakyū ticket barrier but retain your ticket, as you are still within the JR station. Turn left and walk along the passageway to the JR exit. Go down the stairs just outside that lead down to a shopping mall. At the bottom, slightly to the left, are stairs marked "バスのりば 1-8" (Bus Stands Nos. 1–8). Climb these and go to Bus Stand No. 3. There, catch a Hakone Tozan Tetsudō bus bound for Hakone-

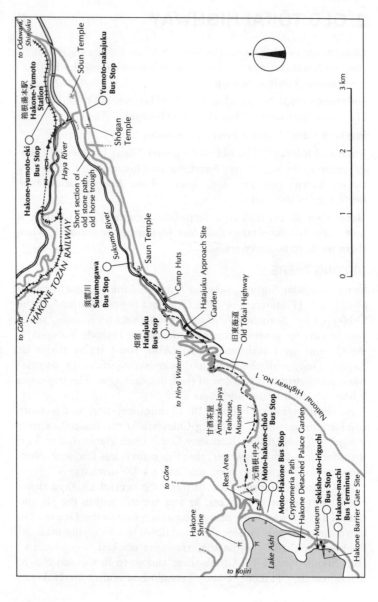

machi (箱根町), and get off at Moto-hakone-chūō (元箱根中央).

The spectacularly scenic journey up the winding mountain road lasts 50–60 minutes, and the fare is ¥1,000 (the fare is the same wherever you get off after this point). If you wish to view Lake Ashi (*Ashi-no-ko*, 芦ノ湖) and its red *torii* (the entrance gate to Hakone Shrine), stay on the bus until the next stop, Moto-Hakone (元箱根), a few hundred meters farther on. Opposite is the pier from where cruise boats leave for the other side of the lake. (This point is also considered to provide one of the best views of Mt. Fuji.) To start the walk, simply stroll back along the road in the direction from which the bus came, through another giant red *torii*, to Moto-hakone-chūō Bus Stop.

A further alternative, should you be interested in seeing the site of the historical barrier gate and the cryptomeria path, is to remain on the bus for several more minutes and to alight at Sekisho-ato-iriguchi (関所跡入口) or the terminus, Hakone-machi, a few hundred meters beyond. This is described in the next section.

Alternative Starting Point: Hakone-machi (additional 20–25 minutes)

Located near the pier in front of Hakone-machi are shops and restaurants, and the waterfront view is attractive. Walk back along the main road to Sekisho-ato-iriguchi Bus Stop, where a road opposite leads in the direction of the lake. A short distance down this is the site of the Hakone Barrier Gate (*Sekisho*). This was first established in 1619 by the Tokugawa shogunate as a checkpoint to control movement, particularly of men and arms, along the Tōkai Highway that linked the capital of Edo (now Tokyo) with the former capital, Kyoto. On the right, opposite the original site and adjacent to one of the former entrances, is a replica of the guardhouse. The barrier was removed in 1869.

On the left, next to the original site, a small path leads down to a pleasant spot at the edge of the lake, where you can rest or even hire a speedboat. A little farther on, also on the left, is a path down to the Hakone Historical Materials Museum (箱根資料館), which houses armor, firearms, and other items relating to the barrier gate. Next to this is Hakone Detached Palace Garden (恩賜箱根公園), formerly a villa of the Japanese Imperial Household.

The bitumen road past the barrier gate site loops around back to the main road. A short distance on, part of the old Tōkai Highway begins to the right. This section, known as the Suginami-ki (杉並木), is a broad dirt path flanked by huge cryptomeria (cedar) trees, planted long ago to provide shade for travelers. When this pretty path ends, continue along the main road back to Moto-Hakone Bus Stop, where there is a small but interesting shrine.

To reach the start of the main path for this walk, either: (1) continue straight ahead to Moto-hakone-chūō Bus Stop, no more than a few hundred meters away, or (2) follow the bitumen road that veers uphill to the right (a continuation of the original Suginami-ki) for 5 minutes to the signposted (Old Hakone Highway, 箱根旧街道) rest area and monument on the left.

From Moto-hakone-chūō to Amazake-jaya (45 minutes)

Next to Moto-hakone-chūō Bus Stop, a small bitumen lane on the same side leads to the temple named Kōfuku-in (興福院), a short distance away. To the left of this temple begins the path. Follow this up the hill to the rest area, where there is a monument to Engelbert Kaempfer, the German scholar and author of *History of Japan,* published in 1727–28. Signs here indicate that this is the Old Hakone Highway (箱根旧街道) leading to Hatajuku (畑宿), and there is a board, one of many, outlining the history of this route. In the Edo period (1603–1868), the Hakone Highway linking Odawara and Mishima constituted one section of the Tōkai Highway (*Tōkai-dō*) running from Edo to Kyoto.

The trail leads across the road via an overhead wooden bridge and then uphill in the direction of a pass. From this bridge begins an *ishidatami* (stone pavement) that runs almost the entire length of this walking course, although only some sections (recognizable by the worn surface of the stone) are original.

This steep section winds through native forest, much of which consists of *nishikiutsugi* (*Weigela decora*) trees, so named because of the trees have both white and red blossoms in summer, and past steps to a shrine. The trail also crosses several roads, with signs to Hatajuku and Yumoto (畑宿 湯本) indicating its continuation.

Shortly after a rest area 20–25 minutes from the start, the path begins to descend, as it does for virtually all the remainder of this

The *ishidatami* descent
to Amazake-jaya.

walk. Other trees along the way are *keyaki* (zelkova) and bamboo, and many birds inhabit the forest.

About 20 minutes later, on the right just past a car park, is Amazake-jaya, which sells *amazake* (sweet saké) and tea. This building, with its earthen floor, roughly hewn beams, and thatched roof, is in the style of the old rest houses that existed every five miles or so along the Tōkai Highway.

Next door is a museum (open 9:00 A.M. to 4:30 P.M., ¥70 and ¥50 admission for adults and children, respectively) with exhibits (labeled only in Japanese) of re-created scenes showing Edo-period travelers and their possessions. One scene reveals how people had to kneel in respect when *daimyō* (lords) passed; another illustrates the interior of a tea and saké shop of the time. In those days, the 500-kilometer journey from Kyoto to Edo took about ninety hours (usually spread over ten days), but teams of runners could deliver messages in just forty-eight hours. Beyond the museum are toilets, and by the road in front of these buildings is a bus stop.

From Amazake-jaya to Hatajuku (55 minutes)

From the tea and saké shop, the path ends after 5 minutes or so at the main road, along which you must walk for several minutes until you regain the trail by ascending stairs on the left side. A sign in Japanese nearby tells you not to feed the monkeys. The path then crosses above the road before entering thick, ferny forest. Along the trail, which crosses a wooden bridge, you will see numerous kinds of birds and butterflies, some of the latter being very large, and wildflowers, including bunches of tiny yellow *sawagiku* (senecio marsh chrysanthemum) in summer. Tasteless *hebiichigo* strawberries are also common at this time, and there are some mulberrylike trees with black berries.

At an intersection about 15 minutes later, the track to the left leads to the road (車道) and another tea shop (展望随一見晴茶屋), while that to the right is a dead end (行止り). However, continue straight on in the direction of Hatajuku. Beyond some rest benches and stairs to the left, the path rejoins the road after approximately 10 minutes. Among the various trees along this section are maples and flowering *utsugi* (deutzia, white blossoms), *gomagi* (*Viburnum sieboldi*, clusters of tiny white flowers), and *suikazura* (honeysuckle, with yellow and white blossoms).

The trail leaves and rejoins the road several times as it makes its way down the steep sides of the Sukumo River valley. Simply follow the large signs for the Old Hakone Highway (箱根旧街道) and stay on the main path.

Within about 20 minutes, you will reach the outskirts of Hatajuku Town. Just before the path ends at the main road is a dirt road to the right, marked "Mt. Benten, Seiryū Park" (弁天山 清流公園). About 5 minutes down this road, which cuts through *hinoki* (cypress) forest, is a trout pond, a recreation area, and a monument on the banks of the Sukumo River, all of which make a pleasant diversion if you have the time. It is also a former stopping place for travelers along the Tōkai Highway.

Continue past this dirt road to the main, bitumen road through Hatajuku. At the intersection of the path and the main road are a temple, craft shops, and toilets. Hatajuku is the center of *Hakone-zaiku* marquetry, which uses cherry and camphor wood for dolls, toys, puzzle boxes, and the like with intricate inlaid and mosaic work.

On the opposite side of the road, slightly downhill, is Hatajuku Bus Stop. The 20-minute ride to Hakone-Yumoto Station costs ¥310. However, since Hatajuku is an old post-station, with several sites of historical interest (as noted on signboards), it is recommended that you walk downhill through the town and then continue along the attractive extension of the old Tōkai Highway to Sukumogawa.

From Hatajuku to Sukumogawa (45 minutes)

Not far down the road through Hatajuku is a sign indicating the site of an old travelers' stopping place (本陣跡) on the left. A few meters up the lane at this point, behind the house on the left, lies a particularly beautiful garden. This was once visited by Townsend Harris, the first American diplomat in Japan, who took up residence at Shimoda on nearby Izu Peninsula in 1857. Farther down the main road are the remains of Hatajuku Approach (畑宿見付跡), where travelers were investigated before being permitted to proceed to the Hakone Barrier Gate. A stone block with a small column on the right side of the road marks the site.

Shortly after, the old Hakone Highway resumes, also to the right. This is one of the prettiest stretches of the Tōkai Highway still existing, with expanses of *yukinoshita* (strawberry geranium or mother-of-thousands) along the sides in summer and large numbers of yellow *kishōbu* (yellow iris) at one place where a bridge on the path crosses a small stream.

Some 15–20 minutes from Hatajuku Bus Stop, the path merges with the bitumen road but recommences 100 meters later, bearing to the left near a small road. This section of the trail, known (and signposted) as the Sukumogawa Nature Observation Path (須雲川自然探勝歩道), is also in the direction of Okuyumoto (奥湯本). Parts of the original stone paving can be seen along here.

Approximately 5 minutes after its resumption, the trail meets the main road again. Walk down the concrete road, which bends sharply back to the right, a little farther on the opposite side. This is marked "Old Tōkai Highway Nature Observation Path" (旧東海道自然探勝歩道). The trail soon veers off to the left, down steps to the nearby Sukumo River, which is crossed by makeshift wooden bridges. Follow the signs for Okuyumoto, thus turning left on the other side of the river and passing camp huts. The subsequent section above the river is very pleasant.

About 7 minutes from the campsite, you are forced to walk along the road again and soon pass Saun Temple (*Saun-ji*, 鎖雲寺), not far after which is the town of Sukumogawa (須雲川) and Sukumogawa Bus Stop. Since to reach Yumoto Town from here on foot requires a considerable walk along the main road, it is best to catch the bus from this stop (about 20 minutes, ¥250). Get off at Hakone-yumoto-eki (箱根湯本駅), usually the terminus. Some buses continue to Odawara, but there is not much point in going that far, since Odakyū Line expresses and limited expresses leave frequently from Hakone-Yumoto Station.

If you do want to walk all the way to the station, it will take an additional 45 minutes. The compensations include summertime white and purple *hotarubukuro* (bellflower) along the sides of the road, another short length of the Old Tōkai Highway, and Shōgan Temple (*Shōgan-ji*, 正眼寺), which has a fine Buddha statue. The stone paving of the Tōkai Highway begins on the left at steps leading down to the well-signposted temple known as Hakone Kannon Fukuju-in (箱根観音福壽院), where hydrangeas of many colors flourish in summer. The path crosses the river and, just before rejoining the main road, passes an old trough (馬の飲み水桶) used to water horses in the past. There are many such historical sites in the vicinity of Yumoto Town.

To reach the station if you are walking, turn left at Yumoto-nakajuku (湯本中宿) Bus Stop, and go down the small road, which crosses the Sukumo River. Soon after, turn right (as indicated by the sign in English) toward Hakone-Yumoto Station. This will lead you across the Haya River to another main road, where you should turn right. The station is a short distance farther on, on the left. Close to the station, but not on the route described here, is Sōun Temple (*Sōun-ji*, 早雲寺), the place of worship of the Go-Hōjō clan, the lords of Odawara Castle hundreds of years ago.

The fare from Hakone-Yumoto to Shinjuku for the trip of approximately 1 hour 55 minutes (by express) is ¥990.

3. ŌWAKU VALLEY ———————————— M

Course: Odawara Station (by bus) → Ōwaku Valley → Kanmuri Peak → Mt. Kami → Sōun-zan Station (by bus or funicular railway, then train) → Odawara Station

Reference map: Nitchi Map No. 26 (Hakone, 箱根), Old Series No. 7; or Shōbunsha Map No. 19 (Hakone).

Walking time: About 3 hours.

Points of interest: The boiling waters of Ōwaku Valley, outstanding native forest and spring wildflowers, and superb views with numerous places from which to photograph Mt. Fuji.

GETTING THERE

From Shinjuku Station, take an Odakyū Line (小田急線) express (*kyūkō*, 急行) (Platform 4 or 5) to Odawara (小田原) Station. As the Odakyū Line branches at Sagami-Ōno (相模大野) Station, make sure you are on a train bound for Odawara or Hakone-Yumoto (箱根湯本), and *not* Enoshima (江ノ島). Also, some trains divide at Sagami-Ōno, with the front and rear having different destinations, so be sure to board one of the front carriages. The trip takes 1 hour 25–40 minutes and costs ¥750.

A slightly faster (1 hour 10–15 minutes) and much more comfortable means of reaching Odawara is the limited express (*tokkyū*, 特急) called the "Romance Car," from Platform 2 or 3 on the same line. Note, however, that this train is less frequent, often requires booking in advance, and has a ¥800 surcharge.

At Odawara Station, pass through the central Odakyū ticket barrier but retain your ticket, as you are still within the JR station. Turn left and walk along the passageway to the JR exit. Go down the stairs just outside that lead down to a shopping mall. At the bottom, slightly to the left, are stairs marked "バスのりば 1-8" (Bus Stands Nos. 1-8). Climb these and go to Bus Stand No. 5. There, catch one of the Izu-Hakone buses bound for Kojiri (湖尻) or Hakone-en (箱根園), which generally leave two or three times each hour. Get off at Ōwaku-dani (大涌谷).

The scenic 50-minute journey up the winding mountain road

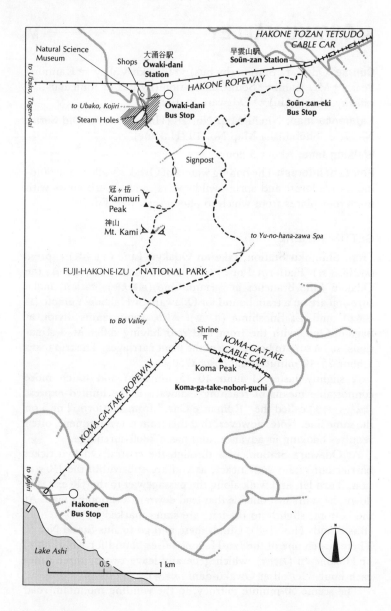

Natural Science Museum

Shops

大涌谷駅
Ōwaki-dani Station

to Ubako, Tōgen-dai

HAKONE ROPEWAY

早雲山駅
Soūn-zan Station

HAKONE TOZAN TETSUDŌ CABLE CAR

to Ubako, Kojiri
Steam Holes

Ōwaki-dani Bus Stop

Soūn-zan-eki Bus Stop

Signpost

冠ヶ岳
Kanmuri Peak

神山
Mt. Kami

to Yu-no-hana-zawa Spa

FUJI-HAKONE-IZU NATIONAL PARK

to Bō Valley

Shrine
⛩

KOMA-GA-TAKE ROPEWAY

KOMA-GA-TAKE CABLE CAR

Koma Peak

Koma-ga-take-nobori-guchi

to Kojiri

Hakone-en Bus Stop

Lake Ashi

0   0.5   1 km

N

takes you past the old spa town of Tōno-sawa and the grand old Fujiya Hotel at Miya-no-shita, and the fare is ¥910.

From Ōwaku Valley to Kami-yama (1 hour 10 minutes)

The white, sulfurous fumes of Ōwaku Valley (Ōwaku-dani, literally the "Valley of Great Boiling") will be apparent both above (straight ahead and to the right) and below (to the left) as soon as you step off the bus. These are the result of gases escaping from the boiling-hot waters of the hillside—a permanent reminder of the volcanic activity that produced the topography of the Hakone area and nearby conical Mt. Fuji. The water is pumped from here to the spas that pepper the mountainside. If you wish to learn more about the geology and the wildlife of the area, visit the Natural Science Museum (Shizen Kagaku Kan, 自然科学館), open daily 9:00 A.M. to 4:30 P.M. (admission ¥400 for adults, children ¥250), which is located a little way back down the road.

A walk across the scarred hillside commences from the large signboard marked in English "OWAKUDANI SPA ENTRANCE," which is between the shops about 20 meters in front of the bus stop. The main section of this path is a loop that leads visitors to some of the more interesting points the gas issues from. Also, there is a small shrine immediately to the left at the beginning of the path. The end of the loop emerges only a few meters from its start. At this point a walking path to Ubako (姥子) and Kojiri (湖尻) commences, the latter being located on the edge of Lake Ashi (Ashi-no-ko).

The basically circular trail described here—which runs entirely within Fuji-Hakone-Izu National Park—assumes you go up the path by the sign in English and diverge to the left after only 1 minute, at a point also with a sign in English. The board here announces: "Blow out. This crater is a scar of an explosion of underground gas. Notice that the underground gas is still blowing out."

A few meters higher you can indeed witness the continuing effusion from a small yellow-stained fissure, and the smell of sulfur is strong. Cable car gondolas of the Hakone Ropeway can also be seen crossing Ōwaku Valley away to your left. Mt. Fuji is behind to your right.

The uphill trail, additionally marked by a sign for Mt. Kami (*Kami-yama*) and Koma Peak (*Koma-ga-take*) (神山 駒ヶ岳) is now rocky and fairly steep, but earth-and-timber steps assist your climb. The path soon enters low, dense native forest with an abundance of canopies of mauve *tsutsuji* (azalea) flowers in spring and numerous singing birds. Before long, the trail runs alongside a small stream, and steam from the occasional minor vent can be seen. On the slopes of this section of the mountainside, groups of bright pink *iwakagami* (fringed galax or fringe-bell) flowers can be found in profusion in spring. There is also *sasa* (dwarf bamboo) in places, and the diversity of trees is considerable. As you climb higher, the view to your rear will grow wider.

About 20–25 minutes from the start of the path is an intersection of tracks. Continue straight on uphill, in the direction of Mt. Kami and Koma Peak. (The trail to the left leads to Sōun-zan Cable Car Station [早雲山駅], 50–60 minutes away, our eventual destination but via another route.) This area is renowned for its beautiful white summer flowers of the *hakonekometsutsuji* (*Rhododendron tsusiophyllum*) shrub. Tiny white "crowns" of *miyamashikimi* (*Skimmia japonica*) can also be found here in spring. Other trees and shrubs throughout this forest include *buna* (beech), *sakura* (cherry), *yamabōshi* (dogwood), *kajikaede* (a maple), *mayumi* (spindle tree), and *asebi* (andromeda). The path splits into two in many places, but don't be concerned—the two branches usually rejoin.

Approximately 15 minutes later, you will pass a tiny spring, soon after which the path flattens out and follows a small ridge with white *kiichigo* (raspberry) bush flowers in spring, eventually passing through a red *torii* (shrine gateway). About 5 minutes beyond the spring is a fork, with Kanmuri Peak (*Kanmuri-ga-dake*, 冠ヶ岳) straight on, through a wooden *torii*. Although our route eventually takes us along the path to the left, a diversion to Kanmuri Peak takes 15 minutes to the summit and back to the fork and is worthwhile because of the fine views in the direction of Sengoku Field (*Sengoku-bara*). On the way, you will skirt a minor, uninteresting shrine.

After returning to the fork, proceed in the direction of Koma Peak and Mt. Kami (which is later also represented by the characters 神山). Again, the path branches, only to reunite. Within

10 minutes, you should reach the summit of Mt. Kami, one of the group of adjacent volcanic peaks that are known collectively as Mt. Hakone. At 1,438 meters, on a clear day the summit provides splendid views, particularly of Mt. Fuji, that are best from the small cleared areas with log seats on either side. These of course also make excellent lunch sites.

From Mt. Kami to Sōun-zan Station (1 hour 50 minutes)

Although the old trail to the left (east) from the summit promises to be an interesting shortcut through beautiful native forest of cherry trees, it is now too overgrown to be passable. Hence, take the well-worn path sightly to the right. This is signposted for Koma Peak (駒ヶ岳) and leads steeply downhill. It varies from a wide, rocky, hollowed-out track to a very narrow, at times muddy, one. White *baikeisō* (veratrum) and Japanese hydrangea flowers are found on the lower parts of this section in summer.

The path levels off, and after 20–25 minutes you will reach a four-way intersection, providing you with a choice of routes. To the right is Bō Valley (*Bō-ga-zawa*, 防ヶ沢), a walk of about 55 minutes. From there, you could continue on foot (for about a further 25 minutes) along the road to Kojiri (湖尻) Bus Stop (last bus to Odawara 7:30 P.M., ¥1,000), on the edge of Lake Ashi. Another possibility is to go straight ahead at the intersection for 35 minutes to the top of Koma Peak, which has superb views of both Lake Ashi and Mt. Fuji, and where in late summer/autumn *hakonetorikabuto* (wolfsbane or Japanese monkhood) flowers flourish. There is also a beautifully sited shrine there. At the summit, you are again faced with a choice: to ride the Koma-ga-take Ropeway (gondola-style, ¥620) down to Hakone-en (箱根園) Bus Stop (last bus 5:10 P.M., ¥1,100), also close to the edge of Lake Ashi; or to take the Koma-ga-take Cable Car (a funicular railway, ¥360) down to Koma-ga-take-nobori-guchi (駒ヶ岳登り口) Bus Stop (last bus at 4:30 P.M., ¥910).

However, the walk suggested here involves turning left in the direction indicated for Sōun-zan Station and Ōwaku Valley (早雲山 駅 大涌谷). This path is relatively flat and passes through thick stands of low bamboo. There are some views where the forest opens out. At a point 20–25 minutes later, the previously de-

Koma Peak's summit shrine.

scribed overgrown path from the summit of Mt. Kami crosses the trail. (The downhill leg of this unmarked track is in poor condition and leads to an abandoned forest road in the general direction of Yu-no-hana-zawa Spa (湯ノ花沢温泉). Continue straight ahead. Later the trail passes through dark *hinoki* (cypress) plantations, then the native forest of the Ōwaku Valley area.

After a further 20–25 minutes, you will reach another intersection, this one signposted. If you wish to return to Ōwaku-dani Bus Stop, proceed straight ahead and follow the signs for Ōwaku Valley. I will describe the alternative here, which is to veer right, toward Mt. Sōun (*Sōun-zan*, 早雲山).

This ridge has some good views and plentiful azalea in spring in its fine native forest. After passing two tiny shrines, the path descends steeply, with many branches that, as before, rejoin. After 40 minutes, you reach an intersection near houses. Turn right, then left a few meters on, and this will lead you the short distance down to the road directly in front of Sōun-zan Station.

Since the bus stop is immediately on your left, you could return to Odawara by bus (¥770) if it is earlier than 4:25 P.M., when the last bus leaves. Otherwise, enter the station entrance on the opposite side of the road and take the frequent Hakone Tozan Tetsudō Cable Car (funicular railway, ¥290, about 10 minutes) down to Gōra (強羅) Station. Note that both the Hakone Ropeway (a gondola system) and Hakone Tozan Tetsudō Cable Car—traveling in opposing directions—depart from this station, so be sure to catch the latter, whose wicket is to the right within the station. It is also possible to walk down to Gōra by following the general direction of the railway line.

At Gōra, transfer to the Hakone Tozan Railway (箱根登山鉄道)—an interesting little train with many switchbacks—for the approximately 35-minute journey to Hakone-Yumoto (箱根湯本) Station, where you should transfer again, this time to an Odakyū Line express back to Shinjuku (about 1 hour 55 minutes). You can buy a single ¥1,270 ticket to cover both the Gōra–Hakone-Yumoto and Hakone-Yumoto–Shinjuku legs.

4. LAKE ASHI ——————————— M

Course: Odawara Station (by bus) → Hakone-machi Bus
Terminus → Umi Flat → Yamabushi Pass → Mt. Mikuni →
Kojiri Pass → Tōgen-dai Bus Terminus (by bus) → Hakone-
Yumoto Station

Reference map: Nitchi Map No. 26 (Hakone, 箱根), Old Series
No. 7, and Shōbunsha Map No. 19 (Hakone) are useful, although
much of the path is not shown.

Walking time: About 4 hours 30 minutes.

Points of interest: The old Hakone Highway, excellent views of
Lake Ashi, native forest trails, and spring wildflowers.

Note: As parts of this trail share the ridge above Lake Ashi with
the Ashi-no-ko Skyline road, it is best to walk on days other than
Sundays or public holidays, when there tends to be more traffic.

GETTING THERE

From Shinjuku Station, take an Odakyū Line (小田急線) express
(*kyūkō*, 急行) (Platform 4 or 5) to Odawara (小田原) Station. As the
Odakyū Line branches at Sagami-Ōno (相模大野) Station, make
sure you are on a train bound for Odawara or Hakone-Yumoto (箱
根湯本), and *not* Enoshima (江ノ島). Also, some trains divide at
Sagami-Ōno, with the front and rear having different destinations, so be sure to board one of the front carriages. The trip takes
1 hour 25–40 minutes, and costs ¥750.

A slightly faster (1 hour 10–15 minutes) and much more
comfortable means of reaching Odawara is the limited express
(*tokkyū*, 特急) called the "Romance Car," from Platform 2 or 3 on
the same line. Note, however, that this train is less frequent, often
requires booking in advance, and has a ¥800 surcharge.

At Odawara Station, pass through the central Odakyū ticket
barrier but retain your ticket, as you are still within the JR station. Turn left and walk along the passageway to the JR exit. Go
down the stairs just outside that lead down to a shopping mall. At
the bottom, slightly to the left, are stairs marked "バスのりば 1-8"
(Bus Stands Nos. 1–8). Climb these and go to Bus Stand No 3.

There, catch a Hakone Tozan Tetsudō bus bound for Hakone-machi (箱根町), and get off at the terminus. The spectacularly scenic journey up the winding mountain road lasts about 1 hour, and the fare is ¥1,000.

From Hakone-machi to Yamabushi Pass (1 hour 40 minutes)

The bus terminus is just in front of the pier from which replicas of seventeenth-century warships and other pleasure vessels leave for the other side of Lake Ashi (*Ashi-no-ko*, 芦ノ湖), a natural volcanic reservoir whose blue waters are famous for their reflection of Mt. Fuji. The lake is home to white swans (not to be confused with the similarly shaped pedal boats for hire!) and offers fishermen a choice of red and rainbow trout, black bass, and the small silvery smelt used in *tempura* dishes.

From the bus terminus, continue in the direction the bus was traveling a short distance to the second set of traffic lights. There, turn right and walk a few hundred meters to Komagata Shrine (駒形神社) on the left, identified by the red *torii* (gateway) at its entrance. Just past the shrine is a signpost indicating that Shira Beach (*Shira-hama*) and Kojiri (白浜 1.8 km 湖尻 10.0 km) are straight on. (This alternative route to Tōgen-dai, your destination, is shorter and less interesting—it follows a forest road through plantation forest around the edge of the lake—but might make a good second choice if you want to walk around the lake on another occasion.) Turn left at the signpost in the direction of the Gairinzan Walking Path and Yamabushi Pass (外輪山歩道 山伏峠 4.6 km).

The old, cobblestone path now underfoot is part of the thirty-kilometer Hakone Highway built by the Edo government to link the important towns of Mishima and Odawara. The highway itself was just one section of the historic Tōkai Highway (*Tōkai-dō*) that linked Kyoto and Edo (present-day Tokyo). Signboards tell us a little of its history: the road was initially opened in the fourth year of the Genna era (1618). About sixty years later, when the Edo *bakufu* (military government) completed the 1.8-meter-wide paving, it became a highway. After the government enforced the rule that *daimyō* (lords) should reside in Edo every other year (as a check on their activities), this road saw a heavy increase in traffic, which was noted in contemporary poems, songs, and stories. The

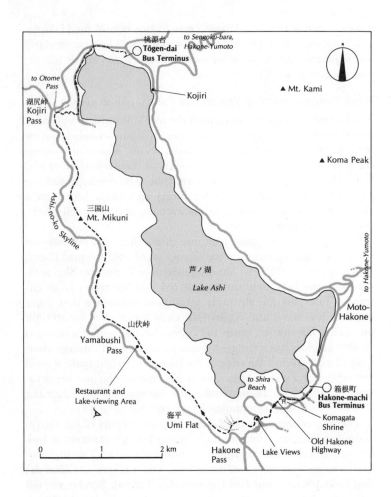

highway was repaired in 1862, and it is said that the paved road in use now is the one dating from that time. The section you are now walking on was repaired again in 1972.

Within 5 minutes, this trail, which passes through native forest with wildflowers and flowering trees in spring, including purple *sumire* (violet) and white-blossomed *sakura* (cherry), passes under a road. Less than 10 minutes later, the path emerges at another section of the same road. Go to the right, downhill, for about 100 meters to where there are excellent views of Lake Ashi. Cross the road, ascend the stairs marked "Gairinzan Walking Path Entrance" (外輪山歩道入口), and follow the path to a cleared slope with more good lake views. Both of these points are favorites with artists, and the second has rest benches and a board showing geographical features visible from there.

Proceed past another sign for the walking path, down the other side of the slope, firstly into cedar plantations and then into native forest adorned in spring with yellow *aburachan* (*Parabenzoin praecox*) blooms. This very pretty path crosses a small bridge and then skirts a spur before going up steep steps in the vicinity of Hakone Pass toward Yamabushi Pass (山伏峠). Ignore the numerous small tracks leading off. About 30 minutes after the rest area, the trail passes close to the Ashi-no-ko Skyline highway. Continue to follow the now-wide, bamboo-bordered path along the ridge (which is the rim of the Hakone caldera created some 40,000 years ago, when the area was volcanically active), in the signposted direction of Yamabushi Pass. In about 10 minutes, you'll pass by a car toll gate on your way to an area with wide views of the lake, near Umi Flat (*Umi-no-taira*, 海平). Clumps of yellow springtime *fuki* (butterburr) are common.

From here the path wanders up and down, again in the signposted direction of Yamabushi Pass, between plantation trees and across a small stream, and then through native forest with flowering trees and home to many birds. Some 35 minutes from the toll gate, the trail reaches a roadside restaurant near Yamabushi Pass (*Yamabushi-tōge*). With its benches and lake-viewing area (complete with telescope), this is a good place to rest or have lunch, and drinks and food are available. A nearby sign warns visitors—motorists in particular—to beware of scavenging goats.

Sweeping lake views near Yamabushi Pass.

The view from here is probably the most sweeping of the larger, southern end of the lake. The various peaks collectively known as Mt. Hakone can be seen clearly on the opposite side of the lake— Mt. Koma with the ropeway station on top, and Mt. Kami to its left. The entire panorama is part of the Fuji-Hakone-Izu National Park.

From Yamabushi Pass to Tōgen-dai (2 hours 50 minutes)

Resuming the walk, go straight through the lake-viewing area in the direction of Kojiri Pass (湖尻峠 4.9 km), away from the road. This old path meanders around the edge of the beech-forested ridge and boasts the occasional flowering magnolia, and it is actually the border between Shizuoka Prefecture and Kanagawa Prefecture. In spring, it is covered with tiny blue *rurisō* (a kind of gromwell), white and purple violets, small yellow *kijimushiro* (strawberrylike potentilla), and many other wildflowers, and there are more lake views.

Past Yamabushi Pass, which is marked, follow the signs for Kojiri Pass and Mt. Mikuni (*Mikuni-yama*, 三国山), taking advantage of any rest benches along the sometimes rocky trail that climbs steeply to this latter peak. You should reach the benches on top of the 1,102-meter-high mountain about 1 hour 10 minutes after leaving the restaurant area. The name of the mountain probably derives from its location near the common border of the ancient *kuni* (provinces) of Suruga, Izu, and Sagami. *Baikeisō* (veratrum), which has tall white flowers in summer, flourishes here.

The path then descends steeply to an intersection of roads near Kojiri Pass (*Kojiri-tōge*), about 50 minutes later. Keep straight, in the direction of the pass, and then down the steps—do not cross the road toward Otome Pass (乙女峠). Turn right toward Fukara Sluice Gate (*Fukara-suimon*) and Kojiri (深良水門 0.5 km 湖尻 3.4 km) at the junction soon after. The steep steps and subsequent stone path lead via pheasant-inhabited forest to the road (the alternative path from Hakone-machi) around the edge of Lake Ashi, some 10 minutes away. There, turn left toward Kojiri and Sengoku-bara (湖尻 2.9 km 仙石原 7.8 km). Flowering *kibushi* (*Stachyurus praecox*, with strings of white-yellow "bells" in spring), cherry, and camellia trees line this unpaved road.

About 25 minutes later, this road meets the main, bitumen road. Turn right, cross the bridge, and walk on for 5–10 minutes to the bitumen walking path that veers to the right away from the road. Another 5–10 minutes and you will reach an intersection of roads. Turn right and stroll the few meters to Tōgen-dai (桃源台) Bus Terminus, just in front of the pier that is the northern counterpart of the Hakone-machi boat terminal. Buses leave regularly from here for Hakone-Yumoto and Odawara.

The trip to Hakone-Yumoto usually takes 45–50 minutes (¥880), but if traffic is exceptionally heavy you might consider getting off at one of the Hakone Tozan Railway stations along the bus route and taking a train to Hakone-Yumoto. There is not much point in riding the bus all the way to Odawara, since Odakyū Line expresses and limited expresses leave frequently from Hakone-Yumoto. The fare from Hakone-Yumoto to Shinjuku for the trip of approximately 1 hour 55 minutes (by express) is ¥990.

FUJI FIVE LAKES

To the west of Tokyo, in Yamanashi Prefecture, the Fuji Five Lakes (Fuji Go Ko) area has an attractive arrangement of five bodies of water that form an arc around the northern base of Mt. Fuji. Around the lakes and on the slope of Mt. Fuji, ridge trails and extensive native forests offer excellent walks and, of course, the closest views of world-famous Fuji-san. On each of the walks described in this section, at least one of the lakes is visible—and on one or two trails all of them are. A vast range of wildflowers and the lava caves that dot the Fuji-Hakone-Izu National Park forests are other attractions for walkers. The area is well served by the Fuji Kyūkō Line from Ō-tsuki in conjunction with the JR Chūō Main Line out of Shinjuku, as well as by a large number of local bus routes.

5. NARUSAWA ICE CAVE ———————— E

Course: Fuji-Yoshida Station (by bus) → Hyōketsu Bus Stop → Narusawa Ice Cave → Kōyō-dai → San-ko-dai → Mt. Ashiwada (Go-ko-dai) → Ippongi Bus Stop (by bus) → Kawaguchi-ko Station

Reference map: Nitchi Map No. 25 (Fuji Go Ko, 富士 五湖), Old Series No. 6; or Shōbunsha Map No. 18 (Fuji Fuji Go Ko, 富士 富士五湖), Old Series No. 18.

Walking time: About 2 hours 40 minutes.

Points of interest: Exploring Narusawa Ice Cave (and, if desired, Fugaku Wind Cave), an interesting ridge walk with excellent views of the Fuji Five Lakes and Mt. Fuji, and a vast range of summer wildflowers.

GETTING THERE

The easiest means is to take one of the two direct Chūō Main Line (中央本線) trains (known as the "*Mitsu-tōge Kawaguchi Gō*" [三ツ峠かわぐち号] and the "*Horidee Kaisoku Pikunikku Gō*" [ホリデー快速ピクニック号]) that run on Sundays and holidays during the warmer months between Shinjuku and Kawaguchi-ko (河口湖) Station, the terminus of the Fuji Kyūkō Line. At the time of writing, these trains were leaving JR Shinjuku Station at 6:22 A.M. (Platform 7) and at 8:14 A.M. (Platform 3), but the time and platform number may vary so these should be checked. Alight at Fuji-Yoshida (富士吉田) Station. The respective travel times are 2 hours 31 minutes and 2 hours 2 minutes. Because the train divides as Ōtsuki, make sure you are in one of the front carriages. A ¥2,200 ticket that covers the entire journey (one-way) can be purchased at a ticket window at Shinjuku Station (but is not available from machines). A direct train also leaves Takao for Kawaguchi-ko Station daily at 7:46 A.M. (see below for details on reaching Takao).

Alternatively, take a Chūō Main Line limited express (*tokkyū*, 特急) from JR Shinjuku Station to Ōtsuki (大月), where you should transfer to the Fuji Kyūkō Line (富士急行線). Limited expresses leave Shinjuku about every 30 minutes from various platforms, depending on the time. The 1-hour to 1-hour-22-minute journey to Ōtsuki costs ¥1,260 for the basic ticket plus ¥1,130 for a limited express surcharge. Generally slower local (*futsū*, 普通) and rapid service (*kaisoku*, 快速) trains that do not need payment of a surcharge depart occasionally from Platform 5, 7, and 8 for Ōtsuki and Kōfu (甲府), which is farther down the line. You can also reach Ōtsuki by catching any regular Chūō Line train from Platform 8 and then transferring at Tachikawa (立川), Hachiōji (八王子), or Takao (高尾) stations to a train traveling farther. From Platform 1 or 2 at Ōtsuki (reached by passing through a ticket gate), travel by Fuji Kyūkō Line train to Fuji-Yoshida (富士吉田). Trains leave approximately every 30 minutes (travel time 44–48 minutes, ¥940).

On passing through the ticket gate at Fuji-Yoshida Station, bear left and then left again to walk the short distance to Bus Stand No. 4. There catch a bus bound for Lake Motosu (*Motosu-ko*, 本栖湖) or Shin-Fuji Station (*Shin-fuji-eki*, 新富士駅) and get off at Hyōketsu (氷穴, meaning "Ice Cave") Bus Stop (35–40 minutes, ¥680).* Buses are not frequent, and at the time of writing suitable

---

*Note that if you wish to visit Fugaku Wind Cave and extend this walk by about 20 minutes, ride the bus (¥700) to the next stop, Fūketsu (風穴, meaning "Wind Cave"), and take the track to that cave. After visiting the cavern, take the trail to Narusawa Ice Cave (鳴沢氷穴) and then follow the directions given here.

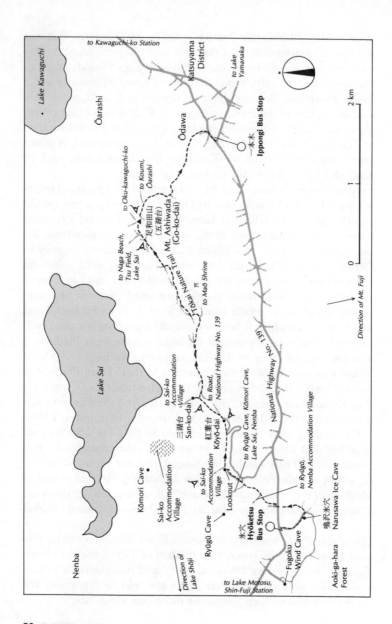

The steep, narrow entrance to Narusawa Ice Cave.

departures included 9:00 (Sundays and holidays only), 9:30 (commences late July), 10:30, and 11:30 A.M. A taxi would be a reasonable alternative for a small group of walkers.

From Narusawa Ice Cave to San-ko-dai (1 hour)

From Hyōketsu Bus Stop, walk for a few meters on the same side of the road back toward Fuji-Yoshida, to a wide, initially bitumen, road. Turn right and follow this road through part of the ancient and diverse volcanic forest known as Aoki-ga-hara (which, incidentally, is infamous for the suicides there). Some trees in these woods are over 300 years old, and this part contains *takanotsume* (*Evodiopanax innovans*) and *minebari* (*Betula schmidtii*). In less than 10 minutes, you will arrive at the entrance of Narusawa Ice Cave (*Narusawa-hyōketsu*, 鳴沢氷穴) on the right. The admission fee is ¥190 (¥70 for children under eleven), and the cave is open daily from 9:00 A.M. to 4:30 P.M.

This subterranean passage is not a limestone cavity but a so-called wind cave, formed by the expulsion of volcanic gases from lava under pressure, as were the nearby Fugaku Wind Cave and

Fuji Wind Cave (described in Walk No. 6, "Descending Mt. Fuji"). The winding cavern is well lit and the path through it clear, although at times it becomes very narrow and it is necessary to bend low to pass through. Because in its lower regions the temperature remains below freezing point even in summer, it has long been used as a source of ice (thus giving it the appellation "ice cave"). The ice is cut into blocks that you can see stacked in the lowest part of the cave. The ice comes from a lower cavity that is not accessible to the public.

After leaving the cave, go to your right and walk along the remaining 50 meters of road until you reach its conclusion at a mapboard that provides a good representation of the area and this walk. Paths to the right (to Fugaku Wind Cave) and left depart from near this point. Take the one to the left. At the fork after 20 meters, veer left in the direction of Kōyō-dai and San-ko-dai (紅葉台 三湖台). This track, which you will now follow for a little less than two-and-a-half hours, is known as the Tōkai Nature Trail (*Tōkai-shizen-hodō*, 東海自然歩道).

The path continues through the always interesting and often haunting Aoki-ga-hara Forest that boasts here some *soyogo* (*Ilex pedunculosa*, red berries and small white flowers) and the clumpily leafed *yadorigi* (mistletoe) trees, and it is wide and rocky. In about 6 minutes, you pass under the main road via a pedestrian tunnel. Turn right and then keep left a short distance later, obeying the signs for Kōyō-dai and San-ko-dai. From here on is the greatest range of summer wildflowers I have seen on a Kantō District walking trail.

These commence with yellow strings of *kinmizuhiki* (agrimony), mauve *hagi* (bush clover), small white *gennoshōko* (geranium cranesbill, traditionally used as a stomach medicine), and white-and-yellow *himejion* daisies, as well as *nawashiroichigo* strawberries and various low-growing *kiichigo* (raspberries).

Ignore the track to the left after about 7 minutes and proceed directly on toward Kōyō-dai (紅葉台). (The left-side track leads to Ryūgū and Nenba Accommodation Village [竜宮 根場民宿村].) From here the path begins to climb and soon follows a ridge where purple *akinotamurasō* (*Salvia japonica*) and *hotarubukuro* (bellflower), and purple and white *gibōshi* (hosta) wildflowers bloom in summer. Another 7 minutes later, the trail joins a gravel road uphill. Spectacular white balls of summer *shishiudo* (angelica) flowers adorn the trail edges. Just 20 meters on, a path diverges to the left to Ryūgū Cave, Kōmori Cave, Lake Sai, and Nenba (竜宮洞穴 こうもり穴 西湖 根場), but continue straight on toward Kōyō-dai.

Although there are various shortcut paths across the loops in this road, it is easiest just to follow the road for the 5-minute ascent to the lookout point less than 15 minutes before Kōyō-dai. There the road ends with a restaurant and lots of chairs for a lunch stop, plus a superb vista across flat woodlands to the western end of Lake Sai (*Sai-ko*)—popular for fishing for trout in spring and late autumn—and to the mountains to the north. *Shirakaba* (silver birch) and *dakekanba* (another birch) trees grow in the vicinity.

From the lookout, take the wide, root-crossed trail uphill to the right toward San-ko-dai (三湖台), ignoring the track that leads off to Sai-ko Accommodation Village (西湖民宿村) to the left at the start. After 8 minutes or so, you merge with a road, only to diverge uphill to the left a short distance later, toward "Summit of Kōyō-dai" (頂上紅葉台 2分). Some 4 minutes later, after passing through forest that has purple-and-white *tamaajisai* (hydrangea) and pink *nadeshiko* (fringed pink) in summer, you will arrive at Kōyō-dai, which has a restaurant and excellent views of looming Mt. Fuji even when the weather is not completely clear. This popular, 1,163-meter-high peak is named after its maple trees.

Walk past the restaurant and along the level vehicle road. A short distance on, take the wide track directly ahead, in the signposted direction of San-ko-dai and Go-ko-dai (三湖台 五湖台), and *not* the vehicle road downhill. When the wide track ends after a few minutes, follow the narrow path that continues, marked "Mt. Ashiwada (Go-ko-dai) and San-ko-dai" (足和田山 [五湖台] 三湖台). The clearing here has a wealth of wildflowers in August: white *okatoranoo* (chlethra loosestrife), red *waremokō* (burnet) burrs, tiny white *tsuriganeninjin* (*adenophora*) bells, orange lilies, tiny white-and-magenta cones of supposedly bad-smelling *hekusokazura* (*Paederia scandens* var. *mairei*), orange *fushigurosennō* (lychnis), more bellflowers, and many others.

The trail runs upward, and within 10 minutes you should reach the large flat lookout with benches known as San-ko-dai (literally, the "Three Lakes Lookout"). The continuation of the trail toward Mt. Ashiwada (Go-ko-dai) (足和田山 [五湖台]) leaves to the right about halfway across the clearing, but go on to the farthest point (from where a path leads off to Sai-ko Accommodation Village [西湖民宿村])—a plaque there shows the layout of the area and indicates the directions of the three lakes visible. Incidentally, since Lakes Sai, Shōji, and Motosu all have the same water level, they are believed to be connected underground.

From San-ko-dai to Ippongi (1 hour 40 minutes)

Return to the nearby junction and turn left, downhill, toward Mt. Ashiwada (Go-ko-dai). Stay on the well-defined main path, marked occasionally as the "Tōkai Nature Trail" (東海自然歩道) and the direction of Mt. Ashiwada, thus ignoring the track hard to the right to "Road and National Highway No. 139" (車道 国道 139) that you see soon after and the subsequent numerous unmarked paths leading off. (Many of these unmarked paths rejoin and form a parallel track that can also be walked.) This gravelly main trail soon begins to ascend again, and summer blossoms along the way include small white *senninsō* (traveler's joy), white-yellow chrysanthemums, and pink hydrangea. Wild roses also flourish here, but they flower a few months earlier, in spring.

Although a path leads off to Maō Shrine (魔王神社行) to the right after some 20 minutes, continue straight on and bear right at the T-junction shortly after, again going toward Mt. Ashiwada (Go-ko-dai). Flora and fauna along this section include pretty pink *shimotsuke* (spiraea), many purple *kusafuji* (tufted cow vetch), ferns, *sawagurumi* (wing nut) trees, and birds in the native forest. The trail remains wide and rocky in places, with some skirting of minor peaks as it makes its way mostly up and along a ridge toward Mt. Ashiwada. At times, good views can be had to the right. Bear right again at another T-junction after a further 15 minutes.

The final leg to the top of Mt. Ashiwada (*Ashiwada-yama*) requires less than 15 minutes, and again summer flowers dominate: pink *hirugao* (convolvulus), orange *kurumayuri* (lily), yellow *nikkōkisuge* (day lily), *matsuyoigusa* (evening primrose), *ominaeshi* (patrinia), feathery white-pink *shimotsukesō* (filipendula), and purple *matsumushisō* (gypsy rose or scabiosa). There are also edible *yamabudō* (wild grapes that fruit in autumn) and *sasa* (dwarf bamboo) on the trail sides. Five minutes before the 1,355-meter-high summit, a sign on a tree confirms your position (五湖台まであと5分), and perhaps 2 minutes later you will pass a trail on the left side that heads in the direction of Naga Beach (*Naga-hama*, on Lake Kawaguchi), Tsu Field (*Tsu-bara*), and Lake Sai (長浜 津原 西湖), but walk straight on, in the signposted direction of Katsuyama District, Ōarashi, and Ōdawa (勝山村 大嵐 大田和).

The alternative name for Mt. Ashiwada is "Go-ko-dai," suggesting correctly that given clear conditions all five of the Fuji lakes can be seen from this point, lying in a northerly arc from west to east, making it a superb stop—and the Fuji panorama to the south is equally dramatic. Lake Yamanaka, the farthest to the east (Lake Kawaguchi is closest), is the largest of the Fuji Five Lakes, while westward lie (in order of increasing distance) Lake Sai, Lake Shōji (the smallest), and Lake Motosu (the deepest), which doesn't freeze over in winter.

When the majesty of the scenery wears off and you are refreshed, resume this walk by proceeding down the other side of the summit in the direction of Katsuyama District, Ōarashi, and Ōdawa (ignore the path to the left to Oku-kawaguchi-ko (奥河口湖). The trail runs through plantation with *tsuga* (Japanese hemlock) and *hinoki* (cypress).

At the fork encountered after less than 5 minutes, keep right toward Ōdawa and the National Highway (大田和 国道), thus avoiding Koumi and Ōarashi (小海 大嵐) (the latter's bus stop [大嵐入口] being about a 20-minute longer alternative finish to this walk). Some 10 minutes later, go straight, ignoring the path coming in from the left and going toward Ōdawa (大田和). This steep descent boasts strawberries and raspberries and, in late summer/early autumn, tiny pink *kitsunenomago* (justica) flowers, as it descends via log-and-earth steps through an unmarked junction and then zigzags down a spur through native forest with *akamatsu* (red pine) and *semi* (cicadas).

After approximately 25 minutes, you will emerge on a dirt track close to a bitumen road. Walk the short distance to the left to this bitumen road and turn right, uphill. Ignore the road veering off to the right shortly after, and a few minutes later you will reach an intersection with the main road. Pink-white *hiyodoribana* (eupatorium joe-pye weed) blossoms can be found nearby in August. Ippongi (一本木) Bus Stop is on the corner to your left, from where buses leave for Fuji-Yoshida Station (富士吉田駅). However, alight before then at Kawaguchi-ko Station (*Kawaguchi-ko-eki*, 河口湖駅). The fare is ¥340, and the ride takes roughly 20 minutes. At the time of writing, the last bus was scheduled for at least 7:53 P.M. (6:32 P.M. on holidays). If the buses are too infrequent or have ceased running, the 5-kilometer walk back to the station (essentially straight along the main road, but you can take a shortcut by walking back along the small bitumen road used to get to the bus stop) would probably take about 1 hour.

From Kawaguchi-ko Station (the terminus of the Fuji Kyūkō Line), return to Shinjuku by following in reverse the instructions in the "Getting There" section for this walk. Don't be alarmed when the train changes direction on leaving Fuji-Yoshida Station—this is simply due to an unusual track arrangement. The fare for the entire journey is ¥2,330 (which you may need to pay as two separate tickets of ¥1,260 and ¥1,070, for the two lines used), and it will probably be necessary to transfer at Ōtsuki (to Platform 4/5).

Course: Kawaguchi-ko Station (by bus) → Oniwa Bus Stop → Sangōme → Tenjin Pass → Fuji Wind Hole → Aka-ike Bus Stop (by bus) → Kawaguchi-ko Station

Reference map: Nitchi Map No. 25 (Fuji Go Ko, 富士 五湖), Old Series No. 6; or Shōbunsha Map No. 18 (Fuji Fuji Go Ko, 富士 富士五湖), Old Series No. 18.

Walking time: About 4 hours 50 minutes.

Points of interest: Closeup views of Mt. Fuji and the Southern Alps, superb native forest, Fuji Wind Hole (a flashlight is needed to explore it), and Lake Shōji.

Note: This walk can only be completed from early April to mid-November, when the buses are running.

GETTING THERE

The easiest means is to take one of the two direct Chūō Main Line (中央本線) trains (known as the "*Mitsu-tōge Kawaguchi Gō*" [三ツ峠かわぐち号] and the "*Horidee Kaisoku Pikunikku Gō*" [ホリデー快速ピクニック号]) that run on Sundays and public holidays during the warmer months between Shinjuku and Kawaguchi-ko (河口湖) Station, the terminus of the Fuji Kyūkō Line and your destination. At the time of writing, these trains were leaving JR Shinjuku Station at 6:22 A.M. (Platform 7) and at 8:14 A.M. (Platform 3), but the time and platform number may vary so these should be checked. Because the train divides at Ōtsuki, make sure you are in one of the front carriages. A ¥2,330 ticket that covers the entire journey (one-way) can be purchased at a ticket window (but is not available from machines). The respective journey times are 2 hours 36 minutes and 2 hours 7 minutes. A direct train also leaves Takao for Kawaguchi-ko Station daily at 7:46 A.M. (see below for details on reaching Takao).

Alternatively, take a Chūō Main Line limited express (*tokkyū*, 特急) from JR Shinjuku Station to Ōtsuki (大月), where you should transfer to the Fuji Kyūkō Line (富士急行線). Limited expresses leave Shinjuku about every 30 minutes from various platforms, depending on the time. The 1-hour to 1-hour-22-minute journey to

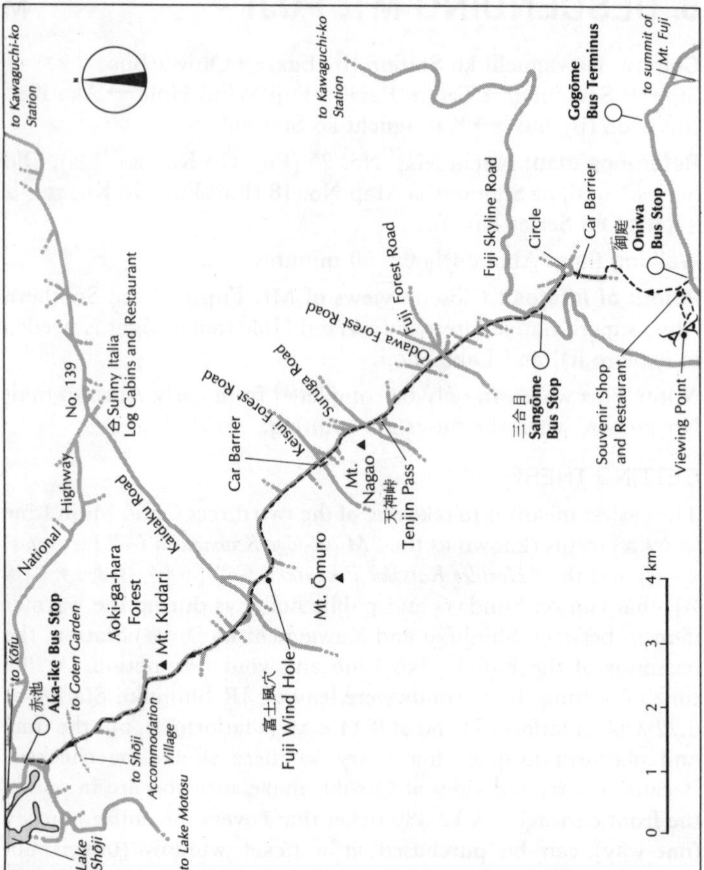

to Kawaguchi-ko Station
to Kawaguchi-ko Station
Gogōme Bus Terminus
to summit of Mt. Fuji
Fuji Skyline Road
Car Barrier
Circle
御庭
Oniwa Bus Stop
Fuji Forest Road
Odawa Forest Road
三合目
Sangōme Bus Stop
Souvenir Shop and Restaurant
Viewing Point
Suruga Road
Keisui Forest Road
Car Barrier
Mt. Nagao
天神峠
Tenjin Pass
Sunny Italia Log Cabins and Restaurant
No. 139
National Highway
Kaidaku Road
Mt. Ōmuro
富士風穴
Fuji Wind Hole
Aoki-ga-hara Forest
Mt. Kudari
to Kōfu
赤池
Aka-ike Bus Stop
to Goten Garden
to Shōji
Accommodation Village
Lake Shōji
to Lake Motosu
0
1
2
3
4 km

Ōtsuki costs ¥1,260 for the basic ticket plus ¥1,130 for a limited express surcharge. Generally slower local (*futsū*, 普通) and rapid service (*kaisoku*, 快速) trains that do not need payment of a surcharge depart occasionally from Platform 5, 7, and 8 for Ōtsuki and Kōfu (甲府), which is farther down the line. You can also reach Ōtsuki by catching any regular Chūō Line train from Platform 8 and then transferring at Tachikawa (立川), Hachiōji (八王子), or Takao (高尾) stations to a train traveling farther. From Platform 1 or 2 at Ōtsuki (reached by passing through a ticket gate), travel by Fuji Kyūkō Line train to Kawaguchi-ko (河口湖). Trains leave approximately every 30 minutes (travel time 49–53 minutes, ¥1,070).

On leaving Kawaguchi-ko Station, walk the short distance across to Bus Stand No. 7 on your right. There, board a Fuji Tozan (富士登山) bus bound for Mt. Fuji Fifth Stage (*Fuji Gogōme*, 富士五合目), one of the major starting points for hikers tackling the popular ascent to Mt. Fuji's summit. Get off at Oniwa (御庭) after about 45 minutes (¥1,450), one stop before the terminus. Buses are not frequent, and at the time of writing suitable departure times included 9:30 (Sundays and holidays only), 10:30, and 11:05 A.M.

From Oniwa to Tenjin Pass (2 hours 25 minutes)

This walk runs through the beautiful Fuji-Hakone-Izu National Park, famous for its large and small outcrops of lava and its *karamatsu* (Japanese larch), *kometsuga* (hemlock), and *shirabiso* (abies fir) trees.

Walk 50 meters or so back down the same side of the road to where a concrete path descends from the rear of a car park into forest. Follow this path, which is signposted "Oku-niwa Recreation Path Entrance" (奥庭遊歩道入口), through woods of low, gnarled conifers. After about 5 minutes, you reach *Oku-niwa's* (Oku Garden's) souvenir shop and restaurant, which offers grilled mushrooms.

Although the trail described here continues straight downhill, you are recommended to make a short detour by turning left. Walk past the small *tengu* (long-nosed goblin) and *geta* (wooden clogs) shrine and then along the paving stones—go in either direction when the path divides. A few minutes later, these tracks re-

Clouds roll in over a snow-streaked Mt. Fuji.

join and lead you to an excellent lookout for a view of the famous conical peak of Mt. Fuji (*Fuji-san*, 富士山). Because you are so close, even on cloudy days the view may be good. There are picnic tables and chairs nearby. A few meters farther, where the path stops, is a viewing area enclosed by a railing, which has a spectacular vista across the plain to Japan's Southern Alps—an unforgettable sight for me. This would also make an excellent lunch stop, if you have arrived here late.

Return to the T-junction, on the corner of which is a souvenir shop, and proceed left downhill (this whole route is essentially downhill or flat). Initially, in this forest you walk over volcanic rocks, some covered with white moss and fungi of different colors. This natural beauty is complemented late in the year by the striking autumn colors of the deciduous trees and a carpet of leaves and moss, and in summer by pale red *hakusanshakunage* (azalea) flowers. Signs along the way indicate that this is the direction of Sangōme Bus Stop (三合目バス停に至る) and Funazu-guchi (船津口三合目に至る).

As you move farther from the snowline (that is, lower), the trees gradually become taller. The soil is a rich black and draws gatherers of the prized *matsutake* (*Armillaria edodes*) mushroom. Ferns and rooty ground cover appear and the forest canopy opens out, allowing daisies and other light-seeking wildflowers to proliferate. *Shirakaba* (silver birch) grow here, too, and the path begins to descend more steeply.

When a forks appears after a little over an hour, keep left in the direction of the Third Station (*Sangōme*, 三合目). Less than 5 minutes later, bear right onto a small dirt road. Walk past the black-and-yellow car barrier a few minutes on. There is a large circle here, a popular meeting point with recreation vehicle owners and campers. Go to the left around the circle, and take the first left-hand road.

Fifty meters down this rough and rocky road, which is also bordered by various wildflowers, a sign for Sangōme Bus Stop and the Lake Shōji Mountain Descent Trail (三合目バス停 精進湖下山道) confirms your direction. Less than 10 minutes along the road is the main highway (Fuji Skyline) that ascends Mt. Fuji, and to your left is Sangōme Bus Stop. Buses leave from here not only for Kawaguchi-ko Station but also back to Shinjuku. To continue the walk, follow the dirt road you are already on around to the right and under the highway. This deep hollow also passes through beautiful forest containing maples. Ignore the various minor roads that lead off. *Sasa* (dwarf bamboo) flourishes on the sides of the latter part of this section of the trail.

In just under 30 minutes, you will pass a number of buildings (the former site of the Fuji Second Station, one of ten station on the way up to the summit of Mt. Fuji) and, very soon after, meet a large forest road. Proceed straight ahead, down the narrow road. Again the trail leads downward through native forest, although it eventually levels out. As before, avoid the various minor roads leading off. Daisies and long yellow strands of *kinmizuhiki* (agrimony, named after the golden Japanese cords used for tying gifts decoratively) dot the trail edges in autumn. After 25–30 minutes, you will walk through Tenjin Pass (*Tenjin-tōge*, 天神峠) and then encounter a larger gravel forest road (Suruga Road). This is where the Fuji First Station was located.

From Tenjin Pass to Aka-ike (2 hours 25 minutes)

Continue straight on, traversing the forest road. Some 10–15 minutes from Tenjin Pass, you will curve past a road that is barred with a chain, and about 5 minutes later cross another wide road (Keisui Forest Road, with a black-and-yellow barrier to the left).

Some 30–35 minutes later, the road forks and you are forced to make a choice, so be sure to veer to the right here. (Although there is a sign at this point, it is illegible.) The forest stands in this area include *hinoki* (cypress), *iramomi* (picea spruce), *tsuga* (Japanese hemlock), *mizunara* (oak), *kometsuga* (another hemlock), *tōhi* (spruce), *urajiromomi* (fir), *buna* (beech), and *hauchiwakaede* (maple).

About 6 minutes later, you will see a stone marker indicating that Fuji Wind Hole Natural Monument (天然記念物富士風穴) is close. To reach the wind hole, follow the path to the left over rocky outcrops and old lava flows for about 100 meters to the signboard.

This cave, one of several in the area, is the result of large amounts of trapped lava gas bursting through a weak outer crust of rock. The cave runs back about 200 meters and is about 11 meters wide in places, with a height of up to 10 meters. Even in summer, the ice covering its roof doesn't melt, and there are a number of ice stalactites. The ice on the floor is up to 12 meters thick. As the cave is unlit (nor maintained or supervised), you will need a flashlight to explore it, and great care should be taken.

After visiting the hole, return to the dirt road, go to your left, and in about 5 minutes you will come to another fork. Keep to the left and, soon after, to the right, and after short distance you reach a main, paved thoroughfare called Kaidaku Road (*Kaidaku-dōro*, 開拓道路). The trail described here continues down the dirt road a little to the left, on the other side of this bitumen road. However, it is worth mentioning that if you are looking for pleasant accommodation for the night, the Log Pension Restaurant Sunny Italia (ログペンション・レストランサニーイタリア, tel. [0555] 23-0254 in Japanese), with log cabins and a restaurant, is about 30–40 minutes' walk to the right down Kaidaku Road, a little before you arrive at the main road that buses run along. The location is pleasant, with private rooms but shared facilities, and the charge of about ¥7,000 per person (¥8,000 in August) includes two meals.

In autumn, the sides of Kaidaku Road have red beads of *inutade* (polygonum knotweed), white-and-yellow chrysanthemums, yellow sheaths of *akinokirinsō* (common goldenrod), mauve clover, and bunches of mauve-and-yellow *yomena* (aster or starwort).

Resuming the walk down the dirt road on the other side of Kaidaku Road, continue straight along this track, as usual ignoring any dirt roads leading off. After 10–15 minutes you are obliged to choose directions at a fork, so veer right. The area has some *akebi*, an Asiatic vine valued for its oily seeds and edible fruit and as a material for basket-weaving, and in autumn purple brushes of *naginatakōju* (*Elsholtzia ciliata*) line the trail edges. Among local birds are *shijūkara* (great tit), *higara* (coal tit), *kogara* (willow tit), *uguisu* (bush warbler), and *akahara* (brown thrush).

The forest to your right is known as *Aoki-ga-hara*, a dense woodland notorious for its suicides. (On average, five bodies are found there each year.) It is said that a number of these people change their mind but perish anyway, due to their inability to find their way out of this bewildering natural maze.

After about 55 minutes of walking through these beautiful woods, you pass a tiny shrine, and paths lead off to Shōji Accommodation Village (精進民宿村まで 0.9 km) and Goten Garden (御殿庭 2.8 km) to the left and right, respectively, but go straight on. Within 15 minutes, the trail emerges at a bitumen road that loops around to the main road on either side. Go right and in a few minutes you will arrive at an intersection for the road to Kōfu, near the shore of pretty Lake Shōji, which is the smallest of the five Fuji lakes. Fishing through the ice for smelt is popular there in winter. Aka-ike (赤池) Bus Stop for the bus to Kawaguchi-ko Station is diagonally opposite. In late summer, yellow *mematsuyoigusa* (*Oenothera biennis*) flowers bloom in the area.

The trip to Kawaguchi-ko Station takes 25–30 minutes, and the fare is ¥790. Some buses continue on to Fuji-Yoshida Station (富士吉田駅). The last bus leaves at 5:22 P.M., although there is a 6:15 P.M. bus from late July to late August. If you miss the bus, you can call for a taxi from the establishment opposite.

Return to Shinjuku by following in reverse the instructions in the "Getting There" section for this walk description. You will most likely have to change at least at Ōtsuki (to Platform 4/5).

7. THE THREE PASSES ——————— D

Course: Kawaguchi-ko Station (by bus) → Mitsu-tōge-tozan-guchi Bus Stop → Mt. Kaiun → Mt. Kinashi → Mt. Tenjō → Kawaguchi-ko Station

Reference map: Nitchi Map No. 25 (Fuji Go Ko, 富士 五湖), Old Series No. 6; or Shōbunsha Map No. 18 (Fuji Fuji Go Ko, 富士 富士五湖), Old Series No. 18.

Walking time: About 4 hours 30 minutes.

Points of interest: Autumn colors and wildflowers, spectacular Mt. Fuji, lake, and mountain range views.

Note: This walk can only be completed from late March to late November, when the buses are running.

GETTING THERE

The easiest means is to take one of the two direct Chūō Main Line (中央本線) trains (known as the "*Mitsu-tōge Kawaguchi Gō*" [三ツ峠かわぐち号] and the "*Horidee Kaisoku Pikunikku Gō*" [ホリデー快速ピクニック号]) that run on Sundays and public holidays during the warmer months between Shinjuku and Kawaguchi-ko (河口湖) Station, the terminus of the Fuji Kyūkō Line and your destination. At the time of writing, these trains were leaving JR Shinjuku Station at 6:22 A.M. (Platform 7) and at 8:14 A.M. (Platform 3), but the time and platform number may vary so these should be checked. Because the train divides at Ōtsuki, make sure you are in one of the front carriages. A ¥2,330 ticket that covers the entire journey (one way) can be purchased at a ticket window (but is not available from machines). The respective journey times are 2 hours 36 minutes and 2 hours 7 minutes. A direct train also leaves Takao for Kawaguchi-ko Station daily at 7:46 A.M. (see below for details on reaching Takao).

Alternatively, take a Chūō Line limited express (*tokkyū*, 特急) from JR Shinjuku Station to Ōtsuki (大月), where you should transfer to the Fuji Kyūkō Line (富士急行線). Limited expresses leave Shinjuku about every 30 minutes from various platforms, depending on the time. The 1-hour to 1-hour-22-minute journey to

Ōtsuki costs ¥1,260 for the basic ticket plus ¥1,130 for a limited express surcharge. Generally slower local (*futsū*, 普通) and rapid service (*kaisoku*, 快速) trains that do not need payment of a surcharge depart occasionally from Platform 5, 7, and 8 for Ōtsuki and Kōfu (甲府), which is farther down the line. You can also reach Ōtsuki by catching any regular Chūō Line train from Platform 8 and then transferring at Tachikawa (立川), Hachiōji (八王子), or Takao (高尾) stations to a train traveling farther. From Platform 1 or 2 at Ōtsuki (reached by passing through a ticket gate), travel by Fuji Kyūkō Line train to Kawaguchi-ko (河口湖). Trains leave approximately every 30 minutes (travel time 49–53 minutes, ¥1,070).

On leaving Kawaguchi-ko Station, walk to Bus Stand No. 2 immediately in front of the station exit. There, board a bus bound for Tenka-jaya (天下茶屋). This pleasant 25-minute trip takes you along the eastern shore of Lake Kawaguchi before climbing into the hills. Get off at Mitsu-tōge-tozan-guchi (三ッ峠登山口) Bus Stop, a few minutes before the terminus. The fare is ¥630. Buses are infrequent, and at the time of writing the only suitable departures were on Sundays and holidays at 9:00, 9:30, and 10:30 A.M., from late March to late November.

From Mitsu-tōge-tozan-guchi to Mt. Kaiun (1 hour 30 minutes)

A little beyond Mitsu-tōge-tozan-guchi Bus Stop, a small bitumen road leads off to the right. Follow this road, which is signposted "Access to the Three Passes" (*Mitsu-tōge-iriguchi*, 三ッ峠入口) and runs uphill parallel to a small river. Waterfalls on both sides of the road, and the fine forest and numerous wildflowers in autumn, including tall yellow *matsuyoigusa* (oenothera), daisies, and pink *inutade* (polygonum knotweed) beads, make this a pleasant climb.

After about 12 minutes, bear left up the dirt road similarly marked "Access to the Three Passes," thus leaving the signposted, still-bitumen-surfaced Nishikawa-Arakura Forest Road (西川新倉林道). Fifty meters later, near a small NTT building, diverge right up a road that is alternately of concrete and gravel. There is a sign here for "Mountain Ascent Access and Beginning of Three Passes Mountain Ascent" (登山道入口 三ッ峠登山口).

The road becomes rougher and narrower as it rises steeply through Fuji-Hakone-Izu National Park forest that includes many

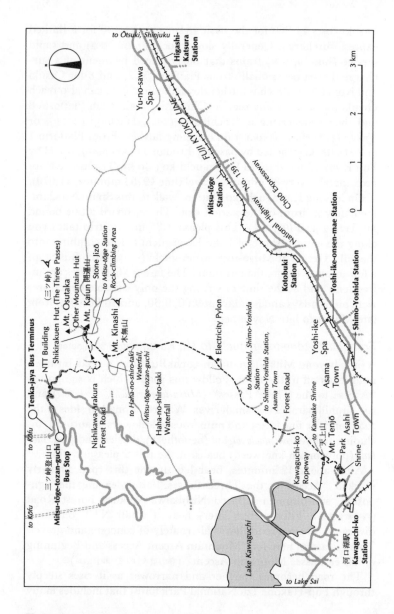

to Ōtsuki, Shinjuku

Higashi-Katsura Station

Yu-no-sawa Spa

FUJI KYŪKŌ LINE

Chūō Expressway

National Highway No. 139

Mitsu-tōge Station

to Mitsu-tōge Station
Rock-climbing Area

Stone Jizō

Shikirakuen Hut (The Three Passes) (三ツ峠)
Mt. Osutaka
Other Mountain Hut
Mt. Kalun 勝運山
Tenka-jaya Bus Terminus
NTT Building
Mt. Kinashi 木無山

Kotobuki Station

Yoshi-ike-onsen-mae Station

Shimo-Yoshida Station

Shimo-Yoshida Station,
Asama Town

Electricity Pylon

to Memorial, Shimo-Yoshida

to Kōfu

Mitsu-tōge-tozan-guchi Bus Stop
三ツ峠登山口

to Kōfu

Nishikawa-Arakura Forest Road

to Haha-no-shiro-taki Waterfall,
Mitsu-tōge-tozan-guchi

Haha-no-shiro-taki Waterfall

Forest Road

Yoshi-ike Spa

Kawaguchi-ko Ropeway

to Kamitake Shrine

Mt. Tenjō 天上山

Asama Town

Asahi Town

Asama Park
Asahi Shrine

Kawaguchi-ko Station
河口湖駅

Lake Kawaguchi

to Lake Sai

3 km

2

1

0

N

karamatsu (larch) trees, various kinds of daisies, and stalks of tiny purple *akinotamurasō* (salvia) blossoms. A series of new anti-erosion walls unfortunately mars the beauty. After about 35 minutes, the road flattens out, and there are benches and a good view, but it soon winds upward once more. Ignore the many minor foot trails (some of which are shortcuts across loops in the vehicle track) that lead off from the main course. Up higher, the vegetation changes and there are more open areas.

At a fork in the trail some 25 minutes later, continue directly on (rather than veering right), toward Shikirakuen Access (四季楽園入口). At this point is also erected a sign in English for Mt. Mitsutōge. After a little more than 5 minutes, keep right at another fork, which will take you to the front of the Three Passes' Shikirakuen Mountain Hut, one of several *koya* (huts) in the area, where hikers can get food and accommodation. The name "Three Passes" (*Mitsu-tōge*, 三ツ峠) originates from the closely grouped trio of nearby peaks: Mt. Kinashi (木無山), Mt. Kaiun (開運山), and Mt. Osutaka (御巣鷹山), collectively known as Mt. Mitsu-tōge. There are tables and benches here, and the Mt. Fuji vistas are spectacular, making this an excellent lunch stop. Alternatively, walk a little farther, take the trail slightly to the right at yet another fork, and then follow the track to the right—just before another mountain hut—up to the summit of Mt. Kaiun (*Kaiun-san*). You will reach the top in less than 10 minutes.

Again, in fine weather the views are superb, with panoramas not only of Fuji but also of Lakes Kawaguchi (河口湖), Sai (西湖), and Motosu (本栖湖), and even of the Southern Alps (南アルプス). A plaque indicates the direction of prominent landmarks. The surrounding deciduous trees provide a splendid foreground in autumn, and white bell-shaped *dōdantsutsuji* (*Enkianthus perulatus*) flowers flourish in spring. Other interesting flora include at least four kinds of *azami* (thistle). The most impressive of these is the *fujiazami* (*Cirsium purpuratum*) plant, whose giant purple heads grow up to ten centimeters wide here in autumn.

From Mt. Kaiun to Kawaguchi-ko Station (3 hours)

Return to Shikirakuen Mountain Hut. This way takes you past a steeply descending path on the left side (which you may not have noticed before) that leads to an area used for rock climbing, and on to Mitsu-tōge Station (三ツ峠駅). Although not described here, that route is an interesting alternative. To reach Mitsu-tōge Station (located on the Fuji Kyūkō Line) requires around 3 hours. The path goes by a collection of stone Jizō (the guardian deity of children and travelers) and more mountain huts, and a branch along the way heads off to Yu-no-sawa Spa (*Yu-no-sawa-onsen*, 湯の沢温泉) near Higashi-Katsura Station (東桂駅), also on the Fuji Kyūkō Line.

To complete this guidebook's route, however, continue past the mountain hut and then, rather than returning to the fork beyond that structure, take the walking path (which you have also passed previously) that leads off to the left. In a few minutes, you will reach the top of another peak with benches and a direction marker, and there proceed down the other side.

This trail runs by another mountain hut and lookout with seats. Walk down the steps, and a few minutes later veer left in the "Lake Kawaguchi Direction" (河口湖方面). This track has paving stones and leads to another small summit with more benches and fine views. The area is popular with rock climbers, and within a few minutes you will pass on the left a trail to a cliff, but keep straight on.

The grassy field you cross some 2 or 3 minutes later is Mt. Kinashi (*Kinashi-yama*). Make sure you veer left at the fork shortly after, toward "Mt. Tenjō and Ropeway" (天上山ロープウェイへ). (The other path goes directly to Haha-no-shiro Waterfall [母の白滝] and—via a later turnoff—back to Mitsu-tōge-tozan-guchi [三ツ峠登山口], which also provides an interesting alternative.)

The subsequent track is a ridge trail bordered by dwarf bamboo, ferns, and numerous wild blossoms: delicate blue *matsumushisō* (scabiosa gypsy rose), white-and-yellow *yomena* (aster), purple *torikabuto* (aconite or Japanese monkhood) and brushes of *naginatakōju* (elsholtzia), chrysanthemums, more thistles, and even a few late-flowering, purple *utsubogusa* (prunella self-heal) burrs. This trail is at times barely more than a rut and consists mostly of steep descents punctuated by level stretches, with the occasional minor summit. Wild cherry, maple, and more larch trees and birds populate the attractive native and mixed forest in this section. You should pass an electricity pylon on your left after approximately 1 hour 10 minutes. Ignoring any minor paths that diverge, stay on the main track and follow signs for Mt. Tenjō and the Ropeway.

About 15 minutes later, continue straight through the junction, toward Asama Town (*Asama-chō*) and Mt. Tenjō (*Tenjō-san*) (浅間町 天上山). (The path to the left heads to a memorial and the Fuji Kyūkō Line's Shimo-Yoshida Station [*Shimo-yoshida-eki*] [忠レイ塔 下吉田駅], which is another possible, though not particularly shorter, finish to this walk.) There is a bench near this intersection.

In the vicinity of some plantation forest 10–15 minutes later is a fork through which you should go directly on toward the Ropeway (ロープウェイへ30分), rather than curving left to Shimo-Yoshida Station and Asama Town (至下吉田駅 浅間町). After a further 15–20 minutes, this trail, which in places is wide and leafy, meets a gravel-surfaced forest road. Take the path to the right just before this forest road, cross the road, and proceed down the dirt path on the other side. A high yellow sign indicates that this is the way to Mt. Tenjō and Kawaguchi-ko Ropeway (至天上山 河口湖ロープウェイ). There is also a sign for Asahi Town (*Asahi-chō*, 至旭町) here, and you can see the town below. Ignore the trail leading hard back to the left toward Komitake Shrine (小御嶽神社) about 15 minutes later.

After just over 5 minutes, you will arrive at Mt. Tenjō (天上山), the upper station of the Kawaguchi-ko Ropeway. Cable cars leave for the edge of Lake Kawaguchi every 10 minutes until 5:00 P.M., and the fare is ¥340 (¥170 for children). The ropeway could be used as a partial alternative to walking, but Kawaguchi-ko Station (河口湖駅) is situated only about 35 minutes away on foot. The balcony area at this station has rest benches, telescopes, and an excellent view over the lake to the right.

To complete the walk, proceed straight past all of this, and then down the steep steps. After about 15 minutes of zigzagging downhill, the trail runs through a little park with surrounding birch trees and, no more than 10 minutes later, passes a shrine, near which are good lake vistas.

Soon after, turn hard left onto a dirt road, and follow this around the corner to the left (ignoring the road off to the right). It soon becomes paved with concrete. Merge right with a bitumen road 5 minutes later, and after only a couple of minutes swing right at the T-junction with the main road. Some 50 meters later, bear left—this road leads directly to Kawaguchi-ko Station, less than 5 minutes away.

If you plan to eat in Kawaguchi-ko Town before catching the train, you may be interested to know that some of the restaurants near the station serve reasonably priced local specialties, among them *wakasagi* (a dish with tiny smelt fished from the Fuji Five Lakes) and *hōtō* (a *miso*-noodle soup with vegetables, originating in the Kōfu area).

To return to Shinjuku Station, follow in reverse the train instructions in the "Getting There" section for this walk description. You will most likely have to change at least at Ōtsuki to Platform 4/5.

Giant *fujiazami* thistles atop Mt. Kaiun.

8. MT. SHAKUSHI ———————————— D

Course: Fuji-Yoshida Station (by bus) → Uchino → Tachi-no-zuka Pass → Mt. Shishidome → Mt. Shakushi → Shimo-Yoshida Station

Reference map: Nitchi Map No. 25 (Fuji Go Ko, 富士 五湖), Old Series No. 6; or Shōbunsha Map No. 18 (Fuji Fuji Go Ko, 富士 富士五湖), Old Series No. 18.

Walking time: About 5 hours.

Points of interest: Spectacular views of Mt. Fuji and Lake Yamanaka, mixed native forest, and Fudō-no-yu Spa.

GETTING THERE

The easiest means is to take one of the two direct Chūō Main Line (中央本線) trains (known as the "*Mitsu-tōge Kawaguchi Gō*" [三ツ峠かわぐち号] and the "*Horidee Kaisoku Pikunikku Gō*" [ホリデー快速ピクニック号]) that run on Sundays and public holidays during the warmer months between Shinjuku and Kawaguchi-ko (川口湖) Station, the terminus of the Fuji Kyūkō Line. At the time of writing, these trains were leaving JR Shinjuku Station at 6:22 A.M. (Platform 7) and at 8:14 A.M. (Platform 3), but the time and platform number may vary so these should be checked. Alight at Fuji-Yoshida (富士吉田) Station. The respective travel times are 2 hours 31 minutes and 2 hours 2 minutes. Because the train divides at Ōtsuki, make sure you are in one of the front carriages. A ¥2,200 ticket that covers the entire journey (one-way) can be purchased at a ticket window (but is not available from machines). A direct train also leaves Takao Station for Kawaguchi-ko daily at 7:46 A.M. (see below for details on reaching Takao).

Alternatively, take a Chūō Line limited express (*tokkyū*, 特急) from JR Shinjuku Station to Ōtsuki (大月), where you should transfer to the Fuji Kyūkō Line (富士急行線). Limited expresses leave Shinjuku about every 30 minutes from various platforms, depending on the time. The 1-hour to 1-hour-22-minute journey to Ōtsuki costs ¥1,260 for the basic ticket plus ¥1,130 for a limited express surcharge. Generally slower local (*futsū*, 普通) and rapid service (*kaisoku*, 快速) trains that do not need payment of a sur-

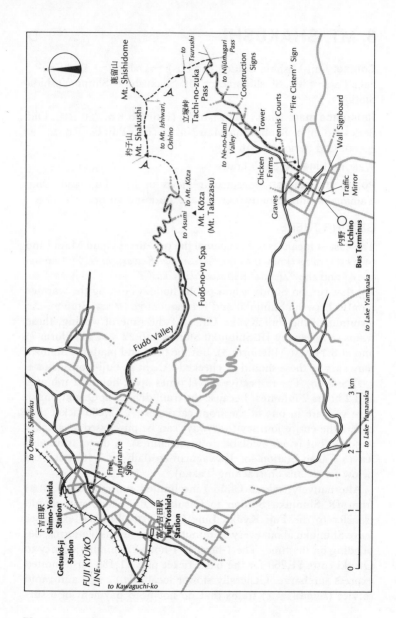

charge depart occasionally from Platform 5, 7, and 8 for Ōtsuki and Kōfu (甲府), which is farther down the line. You can also reach Ōtsuki by catching any regular Chūō Line train from Platform 8 and then transferring at Tachikawa (立川), Hachiōji (八王子), or Takao (高尾) stations to a train traveling farther. From Platform 1 or 2 at Ōtsuki (reached by passing through a ticket gate), travel by Fuji Kyūkō Line train to Fuji-Yoshida (富士吉田). Trains leave approximately every 30 minutes (travel time 44–48 minutes, ¥940).

On leaving Fuji-Yoshida Station, bear left and then left again to walk the short distance to Bus Stand No. 1. There, catch a Fuji Kyūkō bus to Uchino (内野), the terminus (about 20 minutes, ¥450). Buses are not frequent, and at the time of writing suitable departures included 8:35, 9:00 (weekdays only), 9:30 (Sundays only), 10:00, and 11:05 A.M. A group of four people using a taxi as an alternative would each pay only a little more than the bus fare.

From Uchino to Tachi-no-zuka Pass (1 hour)

Turn left down the small bitumen road about 20 meters from the bus stop, where there is a traffic mirror and a signboard on a wall marked "桜荘 民宿桜井 わかまつ" (*Sakura-sō*, *Minshuku Sakurai*, and *Wakamatsu*) pointing this way. About a 7-minute walk with your back to the impressively large Mt. Fuji and past rice paddies will bring you to an intersection with old wooden houses ahead and some graves on the adjacent right-hand corner. Swing right here, and then left at the crossroads with the red "Fire Cistern" sign (in English) about 100 meters farther.

The dirt road skirts more fields, as well as chicken farms and, later, tennis courts. Eventually, it runs through a deep hollow with beautiful deciduous native forest, home to grosbeaks and other birds, on either side. You should pass a tower at one point but ignore the many minor vehicle tracks branching off.

Some 20–25 minutes after you turned, a signpost confirms this is the way to Tachi-no-zuka Pass (立塚峠まで 1.6 KM). (The left-hand alternative heads to Ne-no-kami Valley [子の神沢].) The road gradually ascends, and after about 5 minutes you are faced with a choice of routes at a fork that at the time of writing (though perhaps no longer) was marked by three large construction signs in black and red (the closest of these having the characters "工事中" on top). Take the smaller, uphill alternative to the left, not the larger road that continues straight on and descends. The *susuki* (pampas grass)-bordered trail through thinning forest narrows as you progress up the steep slope for 20–25 minutes to signposted Tachi-no-zuka Pass (*Tachi-no-zuka-tōge*).

From Tachi-no-zuka Pass to Mt. Shakushi (1 hour 50 minutes)

The main track from Tachi-no-zuka Pass leads along the ridge to the right to Nijūmagari Pass (二十曲峠) near Mt. Ishiwari, and an overgrown path proceeds straight ahead down to Tsurushi (都留市), but diverge left uphill in the direction of Mt. Shakushi (*Shakushi-yama*, 杓子山). This narrow walking trail amid long grass follows a ridge on which *ajisai* (hydrangea) flourishes in places. After 20–25 minutes, turn left in the signposted direction of Mt. Shakushi and then follow the main trail right at the small junction a short distance later (a small trail continues ahead but don't follow this).

From here, after a short flat stretch, the slope increases greatly and it is necessary to do some careful rock climbing. Compensations include superb views of Mt. Fuji—when it isn't coyly hiding behind clouds—and, as you get higher, of the reflection off Lake Yamanaka, the largest of the Fuji Five Lakes. In addition, various rocky outcrops make excellent rest or lunch stop points.

Some 35–40 minutes later, you will reach the top of the ridge linking Mt. Shakushi and Mt. Shishidome. This T-junction is unlabeled, but signposts can be seen to the left atop a tiny peak close by. The main walk described here ultimately continues to the left, but go right for about 8 minutes to 1,632-meter-high Mt. Shishidome (*Shishidome-yama*, 鹿留山), where you can lunch or just enjoy the northerly views through the beech forest.

Afterwards, return to the ridgetop junction and proceed straight through this and a subsequent nearby junction, in the direction of Mt. Shakushi (杓子山に至る). (The path to the left at the second fork leads back toward Mt. Ishiwari [石割山に至る] and Oshino [忍野に至る] near Uchino.) About 30 minutes of walking, with an initially rapid descent and the occasional climb, along a rocky ridge with good views will bring you to the summit of Mt. Shakushi. A table and benches are placed here.

A striking light show over Mt. Fuji.

Although a little lower than Mt. Shishidome, this peak provides superb, uninterrupted southerly views of Mt. Fuji, Lake Yamanaka, and the surrounding valleys where the towns of Uchino and Fuji-Yoshida lie. The half-snow-covered image of Fuji from here and similar spots in the Fuji Five Lakes (*Fuji Go Ko*) area is undoubtedly one of the more memorable sights for the visitor to Japan. Even when shrouded in late afternoon cloud, this sacred mountain commands attention with its superb range of lighting effects.

From Mt. Shakushi to Shimo-Yoshida Station (2 hours 10 minutes)

The trail from Mt. Shakushi to Shimo-Yoshida (下吉田) is unmarked but well-defined and commences by veering off to the left from the summit. Due to the steepness of the path, which incidentally passes an overhead pulley system (for transporting logs), ropes have been positioned to assist walkers. The lower slopes boast of larch, red pine, and Japanese firs. In about 20 minutes, you will arrive at a gravel forest road. Here you have a choice of paths to Shimo-Yoshida: either take the track almost directly ahead up Mt. Kōza (*Kōza-san*, 高座山に至る)—also known as Mt. Takazasu (*Takazasu-san*)—and then down via Toriichi Pass (鳥居地峠) (subsequently returning to the forest road), or simply continue down the forest road toward Fudō-no-yu Spa (不動の湯). The latter route is described here.

Approximately 40 minutes down the road—if you ignore its various minor branches, including one to Asumi (明見に至る)—lies the spa, where for about ¥600 you can enjoy the heated waters. From this point to Shimo-Yoshida Station (下吉田駅) requires a further 1 hour 10 minutes of walking, but you can easily avoid this by calling a taxi from the spa's office. To get to the station costs about ¥400 per person if there are four people in the taxi.

To reach Shimo-Yoshida on foot, keep going downhill, past fields and tennis courts, tracing the course of the Fudō Valley's small stream. The road eventually merges with a bitumen road coming from the left. Once in the suburbs, continue through the slightly askew crossroads (buses pass beyond here) and over the river. At the intersection with the large red "火災" (fire) insurance sign on the building opposite to the right, bear right. Shortly after crossing another river, veer left, and then walk straight ahead to the station.

Return to Shinjuku by following in reverse the instructions in the "Getting There" section for this walk. The fare for the entire return journey is ¥2,130 (though you may have to pay this as separate tickets costing ¥870 and ¥1,260). You will most likely have to change at least at Ōtsuki (to Platform 4/5).

CHICHIBU

Chichibu (and its inner regions, known as Okuchichibu) in Saitama and Yamanashi prefectures to the northwest of Tokyo justly enjoys a reputation for fine high-mountain scenery and attractive waterfalls. The trails described here offer walkers some of the Chichibu-Tama National Park's best natural sights and, in one walk, some superb stone carvings. Good access to the area is provided by the Chūō Main Line (particularly to Okuchichibu) from Shinjuku, the Seibu Ikebukuro and Tōbu Tōjō lines from Ikebukuro, and the Chichibu Railway, in combination with the numerous buses that leave from stations along these lines.

9. THE FIVE HUNDRED ARHATS —— E

Course: Yorii Station → Taishō Pond → Magi-no-uchi → Mt. Kanetsukidō → Lake Tsuburata → Shōrin Temple → Yorii Station

Reference map: Yorii (寄居) 1:25,000 Sheet Map.

Walking time: About 2 hours 40 minutes.

Points of interest: Plentiful wildflowers in summer, good views from the site of an old castle lookout, miniature stone sculptures of the Five Hundred Arhats.

Note: Yorii also has a number of festivals during the year, so you might check if anything of interest is coinciding with your visit by telephoning (in Japanese) the Yorii Town Tourist Association at (0485) 81-3012.

GETTING THERE

From Ikebukuro Station, take a Tōbu Tōjō Line (東武東上線) (Platform 1) limited express (*tokkyū*, 特急), express (*kyūkō*, 急行), or local express (*junkyū*, 準急) bound for Ogawa-machi (小川町). The former is infrequent, but local expresses and expresses leave about twice an hour and take 1 hour 20–32 minutes and 1 hour 14–31 minutes, respectively. At Ogawa-machi, transfer to Platform 1 by

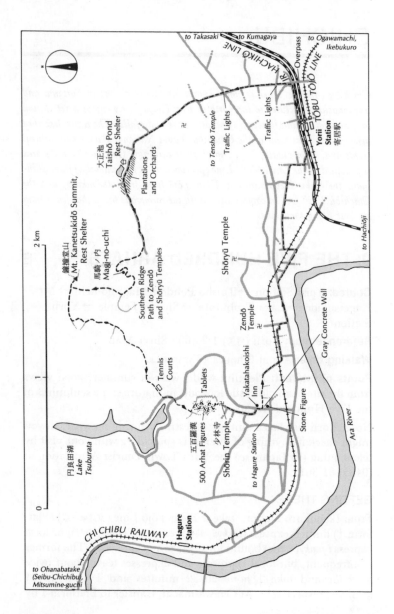

crossing to the other side of the platform, from where all trains depart for Yorii (寄居), your destination and a connecting station with the Chichibu Railway and Hachikō Line. This trip takes 16–18 minutes, and the fare for the entire journey from Ikebukuro is ¥800.

On Sundays and public holidays, Tōbu Tōjō Line limited expresses leave Ikebukuro at 8:20 and 9:00 A.M. bound for Mitsumine-guchi (三峰口) and Nagatoro (長瀞), respectively. Either of these could be used to reach Yorii directly, without any transfer (1 hour 28–30 minutes).

From Yorii Station to Mt. Kanetsukidō (1 hour 10 minutes)

Leaving by Yorii Station's only exit (from the central platform), turn left after passing the ticket gate and go down the stairs. At the bottom, turn right through 180 degrees and walk along the small road parallel to the railway line. This soon becomes a lane, which you should follow the short distance to an overpass crossing the railway line. Instead of walking under the overpass, bear left and take the footpath that shortly after allows you to merge with the overpass road. Cross through the traffic lights and walk straight ahead. Tiny blue *tsuyukusa* (dayflowers) bloom in summer along the edge of this road, which in places runs next to a small stream.

About 13 minutes from the station, you will reach a major intersection with traffic signals. Again, cross over and continue straight, in the signposted direction of Taishō Pond (大正池) and Mt. Kanetsukidō (鐘撞堂山). Some 4–5 minutes later, veer slightly right, then left (essentially going straight) at the slightly misaligned, four-way intersection. (The road to the left leads toward Tenshō Temple [天正寺], as indicated by the sign.)

Proceed along this little road, ignoring the various diverging roads, as it winds slowly between houses up the valley. The area gradually becomes more rural, and the first of a number of *nemunoki* (silk trees) that display beautiful pink-to-white combs in summer will be visible. Various fruit orchards are found here, too, especially apricot and *kaki* (persimmon).

You should reach Taishō Pond (*Taishō-ike*) and a rest shelter on the right after approximately 15 minutes. The pond is an artificial water catchment originating from the Taishō era (1912–26), when it was used for irrigating fields. Proceed up the road, in the direction signposted for Mt. Kanetsukidō. On the left side are some *kuri* (Japanese chestnut) trees, as well as small plantations of *sugi* (cedar) and *hinoki* (cypress). To the right are more silk trees and an orchard of *kuwa* (mulberry), grown for their leaves, which silkworms eat.

The surface of the road becomes gravel as it climbs through native forest, ferns, and bamboo, with a small stream on the left. Within 15 minutes of leaving the pond, a smaller, yet still quite wide, path marked for Mt. Kanetsukidō veers off to the right. Follow this pretty track, which curves uphill through hollows next to a tiny brook. *Hebiichigo* (Indian strawberry, with small yellow flowers in spring) berries, wild pinkish white *ajisai* (Japanese hydrangea), and the songs of *uguisu* (bush warbler) beguile the senses in summer.

The path is a little rocky in places (though it subsequently changes to concrete) and stands of low bamboo flank its sides, as it makes its way after 15–20 minutes to the intersection near Magi-no-uchi (馬騎ノ内), where there is a building or two. Other attractive summer flowers growing here include yellow sheaths of a kind of *akinokirinsō* (Solidago goldenrod), small yellow *kusanoō* (great celandine or tetterwort), and stalks of tiny white *ōbajanohige* (Ophiopogon) lilies.

At the signposted junction beyond Magi-no-uchi, go right, toward Mt. Kanetsukidō. (The lesser-used track straight on is the Southern Ridge path that runs between Zendō and Shōryō temples [道根尾南 寺導善 寺竜正 る出に間の]). This initially steep and rocky trail leads to a T-junction, just 5 minutes away. Go right, in the direction labeled "Mt. Kanetsukidō Summit 0.1 KM" (鐘撞堂 山頂 0.1 KM). (The path to the left is your later route to Lake Tsuburata.) It takes just a few minutes to climb the earth-and-wood steps to the summit of Mt. Kanetsukidō (*Kanetsukidō-yama*) which, although only 330 meters high, has commanding views, especially of Yorii to the south (ahead) and the hills to the west (to your right). On a clear day, even Nikkō is visible to the northeast.

In fact, the site's excellent position resulted in it being chosen in the Kamakura period (1185–1333) as a lookout for Hachigata Castle, which was located to the south, beyond the Ara River. In the lookout, a bell was rung to warn of danger, but in 1591 this bell was removed following the castle's defeat in Toyotomi Hideyoshi's campaign to take Odawara Castle and eventually to control all of Japan. The name Kanetsukidō means "Bell Tower."

There is also a rest shelter here, and this, together with the view, makes the summit an ideal lunch stop. Greenish white bells of *kurara* (*Sophora flavescens*) and small white-and-gold wild *bara* (rose) flowers provide pretty ground cover on the peak.

From Mt. Kanetsukidō to Yorii Station (1 hour 30 minutes)

Ignore the minor trails from the summit and return to the intersection below the summit. Continue straight through, toward Lake Tsuburata (円良田湖 1.2 KM). Follow similar signs when faced with a choice. The path once again becomes concrete-surfaced. There are many views and more wild roses, as well as numerous other colorful wildflowers along the sides of this steep descent. Pink clusters of *shimotsuke* (*Spiraea japonica*), purple *utsubogusa* (Prunella self-heal) cobs, green and purple beads of the *kihagi* (*Lespedeza buergeri*) tree, large orange lilies, and at least one kind of the strangely shaped *tōdaigusa* (euphorbia) are common in summer. Along this trail, too, *yomena* (aster or starwort) plants display daisylike flowers late in the year. A favorite dish with the locals is made by cutting off the tiny young *yomena* leaves at the top of the plant, boiling them for fifteen minutes, rinsing and finely slicing them, and mixing them with rice. Also plentiful on this route are various red and orange berries, including different kinds of *kiichigo* (raspberry), some of which are edible.

About 30 minutes from the summit of Mt. Kanetsukidō, and just after passing tennis courts on your left and buildings on either side, the now-bitumen trail meets a bitumen road. Turn left, toward the Five Hundred Arhats and Lake Tsuburata (五百羅漢 円良田湖). Within a few meters, you can see water to the right. This road has a number of very large *sakura* (cherry) trees on its right side. In just a minute or two, you come to a T-junction. To the right is Lake Tsuburata (*Tsuburata-ko*), but walk up the stairs directly opposite and follow the path uphill, indicated as the direction of the Five Hundred Arhats and Shōrin Temple (五百羅漢 0.2 KM 少林寺 0.7 KM).

Some 5 minutes up the steep slope, which offers valley views and the imposing sight of tall *akamatsu* (Japanese red pine), is an intersection. Follow another sign for the Five Hundred Arhats and Shōrin Temple to the left and then, a minute later (next to a rest area with Buddhist figures), hard right downhill. Beside the steps that follow are beautiful miniature stone representations of the Five Hundred Arhats, Buddha's disciples.

The origin of these icons dates back to around 1500 A.D., when a monk named Sonchō erected a temple in the vicinity. Times had been tough, and the local people were thankful to Sonchō for his thoughtful action. They showed their gratitude by arranging for artisans to produce small statues of the Five Hundred Arhats. Each figure is different, and it is said that if you look long enough at the incredible variety of poses and faces, you will eventually find your own face among them. Their mossy overgrowth and location on the wildflower-carpeted slope add to their appeal.

It takes 10–15 minutes to reach the intersection of paths just above Shōrin Temple (though you will probably spend more time admiring the figures). Although the route described here involves turning hard right, downhill, at this intersection, the path does continue, eventually going uphill and returning to the trail you

Two of the Five Hundred Arhat figures along the path to Shōrin Temple.

were on before. This latter trail is surrounded not by figures but by less appealing tablets dedicated to the god Sentaikōjin. During World War II, people would come here to pray for the protection of this god. After the war, the emphasis shifted to politicians' prayers for election.

Taking the trail hard right downhill, you come in a minute or so to Shōrin Temple (*Shōrin-ji*, 少林寺). Just before the temple, you may notice a group of statues that have been decapitated, which possibly happened in the early Meiji period (1868–1912), when the state promoted Shintōism at the expense of other religions.

Shōrin Temple is in fact the site of the place of worship built by Sonchō, but it is of limited interest, so proceed straight on and out of the front of the pleasant temple grounds and down the bitumen road. In addition to the hydrangea near the temple, you will pass to the left of a cemetery and a *sarusuberi* (crepe myrtle or Indian lilac) tree, said to be too slippery even for a monkey to climb and distinguished by its unusual mottled trunk and bright pink or white flowers in late summer.

Continue downhill and in less than 5 minutes, you will come to a T-junction, with an inn named Yakatahakoishi (館箱石) Ryōkan straight ahead. Go right, which is also downhill, toward signposted Hagure Station and Fujita-zendō Temple (波久礼駅 藤田善導 寺). Although the simplest way to return to Yorii Station (*Yorii-eki*, 寄居駅) is to proceed straight ahead, cross the railway line, and turn left when you meet the busy main road, you may prefer to walk a quieter and more attractive route. For this, take the tiny unmarked footpath on the left about 50 meters before the first intersection* after the inn. There is a gray concrete wall at this

*This signposted intersection has a stone figure on the left-hand corner and is also the turn-off—to the right—for an alternative finish to this walk via the Chichibu Railway's [秩父鉄道] Hagure Station [波久礼駅]. If you decide to go this way, you take the Chichibu Railway train one station to get back to Yorii and then return to Ikebukuro on the Tōbu Tōjō Line. Or, catch the train in the opposite direction to Ohanabatake Station [御花畑駅] and transfer to the Seibu Ikebukuro Line [西武池袋線] to Ikebukuro.

point. Keep walking along the footpath until you are forced to veer right onto a small gravel road, which then crosses the railway line. As in all areas in summer, it pays to keep an eye open for basking reptiles—I discovered a yellow-and-black-checked snake, possibly an *aodaishō*, along this path.

About 10 minutes from the start of the path, you will encounter another T-junction. Go right (to the left is another temple) down to the main road, cross over, and walk to the left. (If you have followed the simpler route to the main road, you will also pass this point.) A few minutes later, veer right with the smaller road that diverges from the main road (that rises to pass over the railway line). After a couple of minutes, turn left at the third small road, cross the railway line, and turn right at the next road. When, about 10 minutes later, you reach the T-junction where you are forced to make a choice, turn right and then left at a similar junction (though there is a tiny lane ahead) a few minutes later. Veer left when you merge with a lane soon after—the station is straight on, just 5 minutes away. Walk up the stairs directly ahead.

Return to Ikebukuro by following in reverse the instructions given in the "Getting There" section for this walk. Trains going in the Ikebukuro direction depart from Platform 1 and 2.

10. NISHIZAWA GORGE ——————— M

Course: Enzan Station (by bus) → Nishizawa-keikoku-iriguchi Bus Terminus → Futamata → Fudō-goya → Nishizawa-keikoku-iriguchi Bus Terminus (by bus) → Enzan Station

Reference map: Nitchi Map No. 22 (Okuchichibu, 奥秩父), Old Series No. 3; or Shōbunsha Map No. 27 (Okuchichibu), Old Series No. 22.

Walking time: About 3 hours.

Points of interest: Mixed forest with fine autumn colors, spectacular waterfalls in the Nishizawa Gorge, remains of an old forest tramway, and good mountain views.

GETTING THERE

From JR Shinjuku Station, take a Chūō Line (中央線) local train (*futsū*, 普通) bound for Kōfu (甲府) to Enzan (塩山) Station. A suitable train usually leaves from Platform 7 at about 7:00 A.M., but the platform and time may vary depending on the season and so should be checked. Take care not to board the more luxurious long-distance trains, which levy a surcharge and do not always stop at Enzan. (The special holiday train [*Horidee Kaisoku Pikunikku Gō*] mentioned in the Fuji Five Lakes section is also suitable, but make sure you are in one of the rear carriages.)

A more frequent alternative is to catch a special rapid service train (*tokubetsu kaisoku*, 特別快速) or rapid service train (*kaisoku*, 快速) from Platform 8 to Tachikawa (立川), Hachiōji (八王子), or Takao (高尾) Station (trains with Takao as their destination have the most frequent connections) and transfer, since suitable trains bound for Kōfu, Kobuchizawa (小淵沢), and Matsumoto (松本) originate from these places. The fare from Shinjuku to Enzan is ¥1,850, and the journey takes 2 hours to 2 hours 30 minutes (excluding transfer time).

On leaving the ticket gate at Enzan Station, bear right, go down the stairs, and continue straight ahead along the road parallel to the railway line. Within 100 meters, a large sign marked "バスのりばこの先30米" (Bus stop 30 meters this way) will be visible on a left-hand corner. Follow this direction by turning left

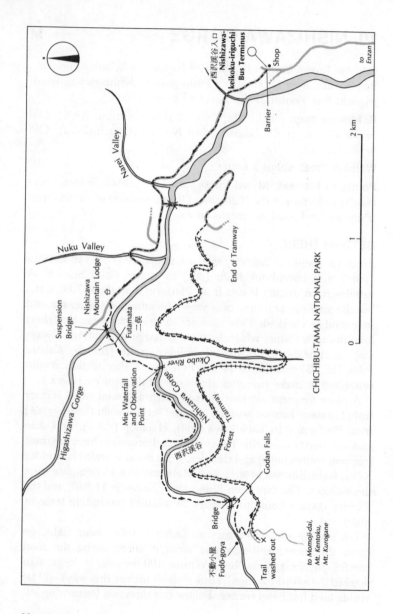

CHICHIBU-TAMA NATIONAL PARK

西沢渓谷入口
Nishizawa-
keikoku-iriguchi
Bus Terminus

Shop

to Enzan

Barrier

Narei Valley

Nuku Valley

End of Tramway

Nishizawa Mountain Lodge

Suspension Bridge

Futamata 二俣

Higashizawa Gorge

Okubo River

Mie Waterfall and Observation Point

Nishizawa Gorge

Forest Tramway

西沢渓谷

Godan Falls

Bridge

不動小屋
Fudō-goya

Trail washed out

to Momoji-dai,
Mt. Kentoku,
Mt. Kurogane

2 km

1

0

to the bus terminus. There, board a Yamanashi Kōtsū (山梨交通) bus bound for Nishizawa-keikoku (西沢渓谷). The approximately 55-minute ride, which passes Hirose Dam and skirts the shore of Lake Hirose, costs ¥920. Get off at the terminus, known as Nishizawa-keikoku-iriguchi (西沢渓谷入口).

Buses are not frequent, and at the time of writing the only suitable ones were at 8:20 and 9:25 A.M. (These run only from late April to late November.) However, a taxi is a possible alternative to the bus since a group of four people will each pay approximately the same fare as for the bus.

From Nishizawa-keikoku-iriguchi to Futamata (35 minutes)

From the bus stop, walk uphill, past the yellow-and-black metal barrier, along the bitumen road. This crosses several minor rivers, including that of the Narei Valley. After about 15 minutes, the surface of the road becomes dirt, and soon after you reach a fork. Ignore the road to the left and continue straight on, in the direction of Nishizawa and Higashizawa gorges (西沢東沢渓谷). Similarly ignore the lane to the right a few minutes later. Gradually, the road, which follows the large river resulting from the union of the streams flowing through the Higashi and Nishi (the "east" and "west") valleys, narrows to a stony, inclined path and crosses Nuku Valley's small stream. In autumn, the leaves of the deciduous trees on the surrounding mountainside are a blend of brilliant reds, oranges, and yellows. This entire area belongs to the Chichibu-Tama National Park, and the mountains are reputed to be inhabited by monkeys.

About 8 minutes from the previous intersection, a smaller track opposite Nishizawa Mountain Lodge (西沢山荘) veers downhill to the left. Follow this, which is marked "Nishizawa and Higashizawa Gorges" and "Godan Falls" (*Godan-no-taki*, 五段の滝). The trail leads, via a wire suspension bridge, across the Higashi Valley near where the two valleys join, and then up steps over a ridge. The point reached soon after, where the trail divides, is sensibly known as Futamata (二俣), literally, "The Fork." The rather inconspicuous track to the right traces the route of Higashizawa Gorge (*Higashizawa-keikoku*, 東沢渓谷), but go straight on along the Nishizawa Gorge (*Nishizawa-keikoku*, 西沢渓谷) path. Thus begins a very pretty walk through a valley as attractive as any you will see in the Kantō area or perhaps anywhere else in Japan.

From Futamata to Fudō-goya (1 hour)

Initially, this ferny path, which in places is a maze of roots and appears to be carved out of the rocky valley side, runs high above the stream. Maple, *sanshō* (Japanese pepper), and dwarf bamboo adorn the sides as it gradually makes its way down to the water. Mie Waterfall (*Mie-no-taki*, 三重の滝), the first of a series of spectacular drops, can be seen after about 15 minutes. At the T-junction here, a path to the left leads to a convenient viewing point where you can take photographs or just marvel at this beautiful sight. The main trail, however, continues to the right.

It is impossible to get lost along this trail as it hugs the river edge with virtually no alternatives, but if in doubt simply follow the signs for *Godan* (Five-Step) Falls. Anywhere along the gorge is an extremely pleasant lunch spot. Much of its beauty is due to the swirling green waters that have worn curvaceous patterns in the solid rock riverbed and valley walls. After thousands of years, the result is cascading falls and rapids, deep pools and cavelike recessions, variegated striations and polished rocks. The color of the water results from copper contamination, and for this reason the river water should *not* be drunk.

In places the trail ascends the steep walls of the gorge, in many instances with chains to help hikers, but it is relatively easy walking. Among the various falls encountered are Ryūjin Waterfall (竜神の滝), Teisen Waterfall (貞泉の滝), and Godan Falls (indicated by the sign 七ツ釜五段の滝). The latter, famous for its five granite "steps" and white spray, is reached soon after crossing a wooden bridge to the other side of the river. A nearby mapboard illustrates your position in the gorge.

Some 45 minutes from the T-junction at Mie Waterfall, close to the place named Fudō-goya (不動小屋) after an old hut site, the trail turns uphill, away from the river. Among the several signs that indicate this point are two labeled "Narei Valley via Tramway Site (Mountain Descent) 4.0 KM" (軌道跡を圣てナレイ沢 [下山道] 4.0 KM) and "Bus Stop 5.3 KM" (バス停 5.3 KM).

Spectacular falls in Nishizawa Gorge.

From Fudō-goya to Nishizawa-keikoku-iriguchi (1 hour 25 minutes)

Stay on this track by climbing the log steps. In about 10 minutes, you will reach a T-junction and the rails of the old *kidō*, a tramway formerly used in the production of charcoal from this forest's trees. The path to the right follows the rails in one direction, although this is washed out after about 100 meters. A little way along this, though, another path heads steeply uphill in the direction of Mt. Kentoku and Mt. Kurogane (乾徳山 黒金山). About 30 minutes of hard climbing up this slope would bring you to Momo-ji-dai, a 1,768-meter-high lookout with good views. However, the route described here follows the path to the left from the T-junction.

This traces the rails in the opposite direction, marked "Bara Plain and Tramway Remains (Bus Stop)" (バラ平 軌道跡 [バス停]). Again, the going is fairly easy, being slightly downhill, and the track is an appealing, leafy one through mixed native forest and with good northerly views of the ridge and mountain tops on the opposite side of the valley. Mt. Kobushi and Mt. Tosaka are two of the major peaks visible in Okuchichibu's main range. Various signs warn of the dangers of falling rocks and loose footing on this high trail, which has in many places precipitous drops to the left, so care should be taken. Along the way are the occasional bridge, the remains of support structures associated with the tramway, and a tiny shrine.

After 55 minutes or so, you come to the end of the line—as indicated by two sets of abandoned bogies—but not the end of the path. When you reach a dirt road, turn left and descend by this to the river, which you cross by means of a large bridge. Then bear right, in the direction labeled "Hirose Bus Stop" (広瀬バス停), that is, back along the road you came on at the start of this walk. Nishizawa-keikoku-iriguchi Bus Terminus is just 10–15 minutes down this road.

Return home by first catching the bus to Enzan Station. The final stop, Enzan-eki (塩山駅), is close to the station—simply walk straight ahead the remaining 80 meters or so. Buses operate until at least 5:00 P.M. (from late April to late November), but if you are too late you can telephone for a taxi. Finally, take a train to Shinjuku by following in reverse the instructions in the "Getting There" section for this walk.

11. MT. ONTAKE ———————————— D

Course: Mitsumine-guchi Station → Kowaishi → Sugi Pass → Mt. Ontake → Mitsumine-guchi Station

Reference map: Nitchi Map No. 22 (Okuchichibu, 奥秩父), Old Series No. 3; or Shōbunsha Map No. 26 (Okuchichibu 1), Old Series No. 21.

Walking time: About 4 hours 15 minutes.

Points of interest: Superb views of the Okuchichibu mountains, and colorful deciduous forest and wildflowers in autumn.

GETTING THERE

From Ikebukuro Station, take a Seibu Ikebukuro Line (西武池袋線) rapid express (*kaisoku kyūkō*, 快速急行) to the terminus, Seibu-Chichibu (西武秩父) Station. The trip of approximately 1 hour 35 minutes costs ¥670. Alternatively, catch one of the slightly slower expresses (*kyūkō*, 急行), the terminus for many of which is Hannō (飯能) Station, in which case you can transfer to a local train bound for Seibu-Chichibu. Rapid expresses and expresses leave from Platform 5 and 7. Note that, due to an unusual track arrangement, these trains depart from Hannō Station in the direction from which they arrived, so don't be alarmed when this happens.

A third possibility is the faster (about 15 minutes less than the rapid express) and more comfortable "Red Arrow" (*Reddo arō*) limited express (*tokkyū*, 特急) on the same line. This is, however, less frequent, is often fully booked, and has a ¥600 surcharge. On Sundays and public holidays, a special limited express leaves Seibu-Shinjuku Station at 8:40 A.M. for Seibu-Chichibu. The fares are the same as above, and the traveling time is 1 hour 28 minutes.

At Seibu-Chichibu Station, turn left as you come out, walk between the souvenir shops, and follow the lane to the left, indicated by the sign marked "Chichibu Railway Ohanabatake Station" (秩父鉄道御花畑駅) around to a road that traverses the railway line. Cross the tracks and immediately turn right, thus following them via a small lane to Ohanabatake Station (御花畑駅) on the Chichibu Railway (秩父鉄道). There, catch any train to Mitsumine-guchi (三

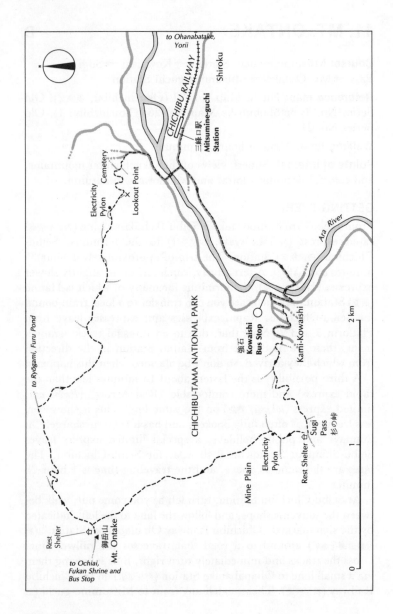

to Ohanabatake, Yorii

CHICHIBU RAILWAY

Shiroku

三峰口駅
Mitsumine-guchi Station

Cemetery

Electricity Pylon

Lookout Point

Ara River

CHICHIBU-TAMA NATIONAL PARK

黄石
Kowaishi Bus Stop

Kami-Kowaishi

to Ryōgami, Furu Pond

Mine Plain

Electricity Pylon

Rest Shelter

Sugi Pass
杉の峠

2 km

1

Rest Shelter

御岳山 Mt. Ontake

to Ochiai, Fukan Shrine and Bus Stop

0

峰口) Station, the terminus (22 minutes, ¥310). You will need to go to the platform on the side opposite to the entrance at Ohanabatake Station, using the overhead stairs within the station.

It also possible to reach Mitsumine-guchi directly via a Tōbu Tōjō Line (東武東上線) limited express that leaves from Ikebukuro (Platform 1) on Sundays and public holidays at 8:20 A.M. The trip of 2 hours 23 minutes costs ¥810, plus ¥600 for the Chichibu Railway section.

From Mitsumine-guchi Station to Sugi Pass (1 hour 30 minutes)

Leaving Mitsumine-guchi Station by its only exit, turn right and walk along the main road, which soon shadows the Ara River. After about 5 minutes, the road curves right and passes over the river. Don't cross this bridge but instead continue straight ahead along the dirt road, ignoring the small road that leads down off to the right near the start. This route wanders through a mix of plantation and native forest high above the river, providing good views in autumn of colorful deciduous forest across the valley. Mauve asters, yellow *sendangusa* (Spanish needles) and *kikutanigiku* (chrysanthemum), and pink *tade* (polygonum knotweed) are among the autumn wildflowers common on the roadside. The road surface eventually changes to bitumen.

About 20 minutes from the start, the road descends to a T-junction. Swing right there and follow this road over the river and uphill to the main road, where you should bear right. A few minutes along the main road is Kowaishi (強石) Bus Stop. Turn left just before this, up the concrete road labeled "Start of Mt. Ontake Walking Path" (御岳山遊歩道入口), which passes between houses. Although you can go in either direction at the nearby fork, the most pleasant way is to keep straight until shortly after you reach a small uphill path to the right, marked "Direction of Mt. Ontake via Kami-Kowaishi" (上強石を圣て御岳山方面). Take this up to the end of a lane, where the trail resumes to the left. The path soon rejoins the road but continues as small shortcuts across the loops of the road, some signposted as before or as "Mt. Ontake Direction" (御岳山方面). Alternatively, stay on the road.

Some 20–25 minutes from the bus stop, the walking trail recommences to the right. At the time of writing this was near some new road works but was unmarked. However, 50 meters or so up this track is a signposted T-junction. Turn right there, in the direction of Mt. Ontake. A little farther on is a rest bench on a level area with views. At the nearby intersection, turn left toward Chichibu's Mt. Ontake (秩父御岳山)—the other path leads to a public toilet (公衆便所).

This leafy route in autumn through plantation and native forest initially zigzags up and then traces the line of a pretty, gentler spur, at one stage passing an interesting earth-and-rock shelter. Take note of signs for Mt. Ontake (秩父御岳山に至る) or, in one case, "直通秩父御岳山へ" (Directly to Chichibu's Mt. Ontake), and you should arrive at the rest shelter at Sugi Pass (*Sugi-no-tōge*, 杉の峠) in about another 35 minutes. There are reasonable views from the pass.

From Sugi Pass to Mt. Ontake (1 hour 15 minutes)

At the pass, bear right up the steeply sloping trail, in the direction of "Mt. Ontake via Mine Plain" (峰平を圣て御岳山). After approximately 10 minutes, the trail flattens out, running along the top of a ridge to an intersection a few minutes away. Don't turn left down the path that within 100 meters descends via steps, but rather veer slightly right, in the direction labeled "To Mt. Ontake" (御岳山に至る). Good views of Mt. Ontake's rugged triangular peak can be obtained from here. Soon after, the trail bends left near an electricity pylon and then continues along another ridge for the few minutes to Mine Plain (峰平), where a signboard has been erected within a dark plantation.

From this point to the summit of Mt. Ontake is simply a matter of following the ridge trail for 50–60 minutes through Chichibu-Tama National Park up a series of occasionally very steep ascents, at times provided with a rope railing. The extremely narrow ridge is actually a spur of Mt. Ontake, and the considerable drop on both sides requires caution—it is not a place for the faint-hearted! Good views abound of the main Chichibu ranges to the west (left), and of Mitsumine-guchi and Shiroku in the Ara River valley to the east (right).

One side of the approach to the summit has been cleared, so

from a distance it is easy to see the *torii* (gateway) and small Shintō shrine there. At the T-junction just short of the summit, turn left toward Mt. Ontake (*Ontake-san*, 御岳山) and pass through the first of the two *torii* and beyond a rest shelter. Less than 100 meters farther on is the tiny, 1,081-meter-high summit, with a superb 360-degree panorama. Next to the shrine is a small bell with a fine resonance. There is also a board identifying the main landmarks visible. Don't become one of the visitors whose rubbish has attracted large flocks of crows.

From Mt. Ontake to Mitsumine-guchi Station (1 hour 30 minutes)

Signs around the peak indicate that the equally precipitous trail that continues down the other side leads to Ochiai (落合に至る) and Fukan Shrine and bus stop (普寛神社 バス停), from where a bus returns to Mitsumine-guchi Station. However, to complete the walk described here, return to the junction just below the summit and proceed straight through, toward Ryōgami and Furu Pond (*Furu-ike*) (両神 古池). The beautiful native forest is ideal for witnessing the full range of autumn leaf hues, and it boasts cherry and maple trees.

Stay on the main path, most of which is steeply downhill—initially in a zigzag—although it generally clings to the spur or top of the ridge. At the junction encountered after 20–25 minutes, go right, away from Ryōgami and Furu Pond and toward Mitsumine-guchi (三峰口). The trail, often bordered with *sasa* (dwarf bamboo), leads through various plantations and skirts several clearings.

Some 30–35 minutes later, continue straight through the junction—again toward Mitsumine-guchi. Once more there are fine views of the Ara River valley, as the trail descends rapidly through native undergrowth home to many birds. Keep on the main path, ignoring the many minor tracks branching off (most of which later rejoin the main trail). You should pass another steel pylon after 10–15 minutes and, soon after, a short diversion to a lookout point.

The trail then winds down to a terraced cemetery approximately 5 minutes away. Between two tombs, a small trail branches off to the right. A white plastic post clearly marks this point.

Although you can go either way, take the small path—a short-cut—down over a tiny stream and past a temple and more graves, and after a few minutes you meet a bitumen road. Veer to the right and follow this road downhill, with larger roads merging from the left in two places.

In five minutes, you will reach a bridge to the left that spans the Ara River. Bear left, crossing the bridge, and stroll the remaining 7 minutes or so back along the main road to Mitsumine-guchi Station.

Return to Ikebukuro by following in reverse the instructions in the "Getting There" section for this walk.

Summer sheath of *okatoranoo*.

12. DAIBOSATSU PASS ————— D

Course: Enzan Station (by bus) → Daibosatsu-tozan-guchi Bus Terminus → Marukawa Pass → Daibosatsu Peak → Kaminari Rock → Daibosatsu Pass → Kami-Nikkawa Pass → Daibosatsu-tozan-guchi Bus Stop (by bus) → Enzan Station

Reference map: Nitchi Maps Nos. 21 (Okutama, 奥多摩) and 22 (Okuchichibu, 奥秩父), Old Series Nos. 2 and 3, respectively; or Shōbunsha Map No. 23 (Daibosatsu renrei, 大菩薩連嶺), Old Series No. 23.

Walking time: About 5 hours 30 minutes.

Points of interest: Frequent spectacular panoramas of Mt. Fuji and the Southern Alps, native beech forest and numerous spring and summer wildflowers in the western part of the Chichibu-Tama National Park.

GETTING THERE

From JR Shinjuku Station, take a Chūō Line (中央線) local train (*futsū*, 普通) bound for Kōfu (甲府) to Enzan (塩山) Station. A suitable train usually leaves from Platform 7 at about 7:00 A.M., but the platform and time may vary depending on the season and so should be checked. Take care not to board the more luxurious long-distance trains, which levy a surcharge and do not always stop at Enzan. (The special holiday train [*Horidee Kaisoku Pikunikku Gō*] mentioned in the Fuji Five Lakes section is also suitable, but make sure you are in one of the rear carriages.)

A more frequent alternative is to catch a special rapid service train (*tokubetsu kaisoku*, 特別快速) or rapid service train (*kaisoku*, 快速) from Platform 8 to Tachikawa (立川), Hachiōji (八王子), or Takao (高尾) Station (trains with Takao as their destination have the most frequent connections) and transfer, since suitable trains bound for Kōfu, Kobuchizawa (小淵沢), and Matsumoto (松本) originate from these places. The fare from Shinjuku to Enzan is ¥1,850, and the journey takes 2 hours to 2 hours 30 minutes (excluding transfer time).

On leaving the ticket gate at Enzan Station, bear right, go down the stairs, and continue straight ahead along the road

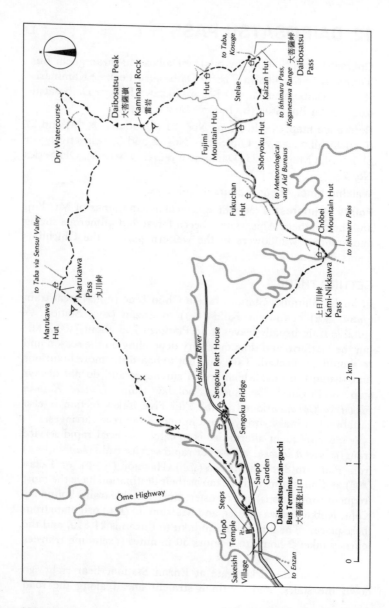

parallel to the railway line. Within 100 meters, a large sign marked "バスのりばこの先30米" (Bus stop 30 meters this way) will be visible on a left-hand corner. Follow this direction by turning left to the bus terminus. There, board a Yamanashi Kōtsū (山梨交通) bus bound for Daibosatsu-tozan-guchi (大菩薩登山口). The approximately 25-minute ride takes you through pleasant semirural countryside and up a valley surrounded by rugged mountains. Get off at the terminus (fare ¥460). Buses are not frequent, and at the time of writing the most suitable ones were at 7:28, 9:25, and 10:55 A.M. A taxi would certainly be a reasonable alternative for a group of four.

From Daibosatsu-tozan-guchi to Marukawa Pass (1 hour 50 minutes)

From the bus stop, which is within Sakeishi Village, follow the small bitumen road (marked "Daibosatsu Pass" [大菩薩峠]) that leads uphill. Ignore the road to the right to Enzan City (塩山市内). In addition to the many roadside gardens along this stretch, wildflowers abound. In early summer, these include yellow *hahakogusa* (gnaphalium cottonweed), *nigana* (ixeris), *tanpopo* (dandelion), sweet-smelling yellow and white Japanese honeysuckle, small white and gold *himejion* (daisy fleabane), and the ubiquitous (and with a reputation of being bad-smelling) white *dokudami* (*Houttuynia cordata*). (A decoction made from the *dokudami* herb has traditionally been used in Japan to treat stomach ailments and diarrhea.)

Within a few minutes, you will reach the stone path and then the stone steps leading up to Unpō Temple (*Unpō-ji*, 雲峰寺). If you are interested in making a diversion to see the temple, climb the steps and walk through the entrance gate and up to the main buildings, which are thatched, and the bell platform. The temple was first constructed in 745 and was later patronized by the powerful Takeda family. Despite the Tokugawa defeat of the Takedas in 1582, the temple retained some family treasures, including the Takeda battle flag. The oldest Japanese *hinomaru* flag (the well-known red circle on a white background) is kept there.

Return to the road by taking the driveway downhill from the temple's information board. Continue up the road, which follows the course of a small stream in the Ashikura River valley and crosses over it. Other wildflowers to be found on the roadside in summer are bushes of white *utsugi* (deutzia), and bright purple *azami* (thistles) and *mushitorinadeshiko* (catchfly). This way also winds past Sanpō Garden (サンポー苑) on the right and a stone masonry works on the left.

The roadside brush eventually gives way to tree-lined shade, and shortly after (about 15 minutes from the temple) a dirt road veers off to the left. Take this road and then the uphill walking path to the right after a further 50 meters. This direction is labeled as "Marukawa Pass 90 minutes" (丸川峠90分). (The bitumen road extends uphill in the direction of Daibosatsu Pass [大菩薩峠2時間30分].) The early part of the trail is characterized in summer by masses of mauve *koajisai* (*Hydrangea hirta*), small white-and-gold *terihanoibara* roses, and, to a lesser extent, the yellow berries of the *momijiichigo* raspberry. The trail, which follows another stream far below, quickly narrows and after 8–10 minutes runs briefly next to the road before actually joining it. Follow the road upstream past a series of water erosion-control weirs until, less than 10 minutes later, you reach a small path leading uphill to the left. Take this track, which is signposted for Marukawa Pass (*Marukawa-tōge*, 丸川峠).

The path then climbs steeply through thick native forest along a narrow ridge bordered with *sasa* (dwarf bamboo) and some ferns and wild pink *tsutsuji* (azalea). The diversity of these woods is impressive: besides the *buna* (beech) and *mizunara* (oak) that dominate, *sugi* (cedar), *akamatsu* (pine), *iramomi* (*Picea bicolor*), *kuri* (Japanese chestnut), and *kometsuga* (hemlock) flourish. Butterflies, birds, fungi, and caterpillars complete this picture of nature at its most attractive. In summer, along this section I have also seen the *yamakagashi* (ring snake), whose distinctive yellow head and red-and-black-checked body allow ready identification.

After about 30 minutes, you pass a major descending trail to the right, which is blocked off, but ignore this and keep going by following the main track up to the left. Although this, at times rocky, path levels off occasionally, it generally remains steep until 35–40 minutes later, when it flattens out just before Marukawa Pass. Here the path flanks open out into glorious hillsides of pink and red azaleas. To your rear is the first of a series of spectacular views of Mt. Fuji on this walk. Even in June, this majestic peak often retains its snowy mantle.

A little over 5 minutes later, you will reach the pass, where there is the run-down *Marukawa-sō* (Marukawa Mountain Hut), the first of many along this route, with very rudimentary accommodation and picnic tables and chairs, and an intersection of paths. This is a superb lunch site, with many wildflowers (among them, *amadokoro* [a polygonatum lily]), plenty of large rocks to sit on, and an extensive view of the beautiful cone of Mt. Fuji.

From Marukawa Pass to Daibosatsu Pass (1 hour 40 minutes)

From Marukawa Pass, take the uphill path to the right, just before the mountain hut. This way is signposted for Daibosatsu Peak (*Daibosatsu-mine*, 大菩薩峠). (The flat path straight ahead leads in the direction of Taba via Sensui Valley [丹波方面 (泉水谷を至て)]). Ignore the large but little-used and unmarked path to the left after about 5 minutes.

Again, the pretty ridge trail is generally steep, but short level sections give some respite, and where breaks occur in the forest there are valley views toward Enzan to the right and the ranges to the left. The large, precipitously uphill "trail" encountered after about 35 minutes is, in fact, a usually dry watercourse and not a track. Ignore any minor tracks leading off this route, which also passes a small spring under a rock.

Some 20–25 minutes later (about 5 minutes beyond a sign indicating that you are now on Daibosatsu's Northern Ridge [大菩薩北尾根]), you will reach the summit of Daibosatsu Peak. Although at 2,057 meters, the view should be good, vegetation obscures it and there is little reason to stop here. From this point, the going becomes much easier and is almost entirely downhill.

Continuing down the other side of Daibosatsu Peak, in about 5 minutes you arrive at Kaminari (literally, "Thunder") Rock (*Kaminari-iwa*, 雷岩), a craggy open section of this ridge trail. In clear weather the view to the right here and farther along the path is no less than breathtaking, with a panoramic view of Mt. Fuji to the southwest and the Southern Alps beyond.

Go straight along the ridge trail, climbing over the stony top of Kaminari Rock, toward Taba, Kosuge, and Daibosatsu Pass (丹波

On the climb to
Unpō Temple.

小菅 大菩薩峠). (There is also a not very noticeable track that leads down to the right to Fukuchan Hut via Karamatsu Ridge (唐松尾根を至て 福ちゃん荘へ). This might shorten the course by perhaps 30 minutes, although I have not tried it.) From here, the extension of the trail across a series of small peaks linked by ridges is clearly visible, and the superb vistas of Mt. Fuji, as well as of open sub-alpine meadows and forested valleys, continue.

After approximately 7 minutes, there is a signpost for the New Fujimi Trail "with chains" (富士見新道 クサリ場コース) to the right, but keep going straight, down the rocky ridge in the direction of Daibosatsu Pass (*Daibosatsu-tōge*, 大菩薩峠). Azaleas and many kinds of birds are common along this stretch, and you will pass a mountain hut at a place called Sai-no-kawara (さいの河原), which hikers may use without charge. Ignore any minor paths leading off, especially to the left.

Some 15–20 minutes from the previous intersection, the marked trail swings left on top of a small peak and then descends steeply, with a hut visible in the distance and views to either side of the ridge. After passing three stelae and a small monument, you will reach Daibosatsu Pass and Kaizan Hut in less than 10 minutes. The hut is named after Nakazato Kaizan, who wrote the famous novel *Daibosatsu Tōge*. This is a good place to rest, and the hut sells refreshments and souvenirs.

From Daibosatsu Pass to Daibosatsu-tozan-guchi (2 hours)

Proceed straight ahead past the hut, in the direction signposted for Ishimaru Pass and Koganesawa Range, and Sakeishi and Enzan (石丸峠 小金沢連嶺, 裂石 塩山). (The trail to the left leads to Taba and Kosuge [丹波 小菅].) Immediately past the hut, turn right downhill (Ishimaru Pass and Koganesawa Range are straight on, up the ridge), which is the direction of Sakeishi, where Daibosatsu-tozan-guchi Bus Terminus is located. This wide and easy dirt track continues for 20–25 minutes and then crosses a small stream to join a concrete road that starts near Shōryoku Hut.

The road initially climbs but soon levels off and descends, a few minutes later passing another hut (*Fujimi-sō* [Fujimi Mountain Hut], where the other end of the New Fujimi Trail joins the road) before reaching the Fukuchan Hut complex after a couple more minutes. The path from Kaminari Rock joins the road just before the hut. Just beyond the hut's tables and chairs, a path to Sakeishi via Kami-Nikkawa Pass (上日川峠を圣て裂石), your next destination, turns off to the right. However, as this merely shadows the road, which is itself quiet and pleasant, you may as well stay on the road for 10 minutes to the pass. Minor trails connect the road and path to the right, and a larger track leads off to Daibosatsu Meteorological and Aid Bureaus (大菩薩気象援助局入口) to the left.

At Kami-Nikkawa Pass, there is a major intersection of roads and Chōbei Mountain Hut, which has tables and chairs made of cable drums of different sizes. The way to the left is to Ishimaru Pass (*Ishimaru-tōge*, 石丸峠), but go right toward Sakeishi and Enzan (裂石 塩山). Within a few feet, the trail resumes, veering off to the left and marked "Enzan Station via Sakeishi" (裂石を圣て塩山駅). It is possible, though longer, to return to the bus terminus via the bitumen road, but the trail is the more pleasant alternative. This section of the road does, however, boast numerous shrub flowers in summer, among them purple crowns of tiny *kuroichigo* (a kind of raspberry) stars, deutzia, and white-yellow *kogomeutsugi* (*Stephanandra incisa*), as well as the usual white *shirotsumekusa* (Dutch clover). By road, it will take you about 1 hour 40 minutes to reach the bus stop simply by following the main thoroughfare. The steeper walking path requires about 1 hour 20 minutes—when you meet the road after crossing the river at Sengoku Bridge (千石橋) near Sengoku Rest House (千石茶屋), veer left and follow it downhill. In either case, you will pass the road and path you initially turned up to commence the climb to Marukawa Pass earlier in the day, and you will eventually complete the walk at Daibosatsu-tozan-guchi Bus Terminus from where you began.

Return home by catching the bus to Enzan Station. At the time of writing, the last bus left at 7:30 P.M. Get off at the final stop, Enzan (塩山), and walk the remaining 100 meters or so straight ahead to the station. Take a train to Shinjuku by following in reverse the instructions in the "Getting There" section for this walk description. Trains heading in the Shinjuku direction leave from Platform 2 and 3 of Enzan Station.

NIKKŌ

Tochigi Prefecture's famous Nikkō National Park to the north of Tokyo could justifiably be called a walker's paradise, a true jewel in the Kantō District's crown. Blessed with outstanding natural beauty, this highland area was once a religious center. The remaining shrines and temples are among the most outstanding in Japan and give substance to the numerous superlatives writers have used to describe Nikkō. There are also many unusual and interesting festivals in Nikkō, among them the Thousand Warriors Parade. The trails described here offer superb mountain views, lakeside walks, alpine wildflowers and ancient forest, stunning river scenery, and hot springs, all in close proximity to some of Japan's finest examples of religious art. Access to the area is best provided by the Tōbu Nikkō Line from Asakusa in Tokyo.

13. KIRIFURI HIGHLAND ———— M
(or E, if shortened)

Course: Tōbu-Nikkō Station (by bus) → Kirifuri-kōgen Bus Terminus → Ō Mountain → Neko Flat → Tsutsuji Hill → Kirifuri-no-taki-iriguchi Bus Stop (by bus) → Tōbu-Nikkō Station.

Reference map: Nitchi Map No. 30 (Okunikkō Okukinu, 奥日光 奥鬼怒), Old Series No. 8; or Shōbunsha Map No. 31 (Nikkō, 日光), Old Series No. 43.

Walking time: About 2 hours 50 minutes (or 2 hours 20 minutes with the shortened alternative).

Points of interest: Numerous summer and alpine wildflowers, beautiful native forest and riverside trails, Matsukura Waterfall.

Note: The bus used to get to the beginning of this walk only operates from late April to early November.

GETTING THERE

At Asakusa Station (Platform 3 or 5), board a Tōbu Nikkō Line

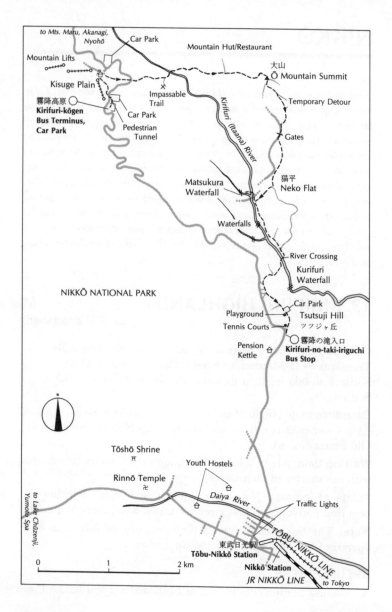

to Mts. Maru, Akanagi, Nyohō

Car Park

Mountain Hut/Restaurant

Mountain Lifts

大山
Ō Mountain Summit

Kisuge Plain

Impassable Trail

Temporary Detour

霧降高原
Kirifuri-kōgen Bus Terminus, Car Park

Car Park

Pedestrian Tunnel

Kirifuri (Itaanai River)

Gates

猫平
Neko Flat

Matsukura Waterfall

Waterfalls

River Crossing

Kurifuri Waterfall

NIKKŌ NATIONAL PARK

Car Park

Playground

Tsutsuji Hill
ツツジヶ丘

Tennis Courts

Pension Kettle

霧降の滝入口
Kirifuri-no-taki-iriguchi Bus Stop

N

Tōshō Shrine

Youth Hostels

Rinnō Temple

Daiya River

Traffic Lights

to Lake Chūzenji, Yumoto Spa

TŌBU-NIKKŌ LINE

東武日光駅
Tōbu-Nikkō Station

Nikkō Station

JR NIKKŌ LINE

to Tokyo

0   1   2 km

(東武日光線) rapid service train (*kaisoku*, 快速) bound for Tōbu-Nikkō (東武日光) Station. At the time of writing, such trains were leaving daily at 6:20, 7:10, 8:10, 9:10, and 10:20 A.M. As some separate at Shimo-Imaichi (下今市) Station, with the rear carriages going to Kinugawa (鬼怒川), be sure to board one of the front two carriages. Alight at the terminus. Seats can be reserved (for an additional ¥1,030) on the similar but less-frequent expresses (*kyūkō*, 急行), although you may have to change at Shimo-Imaichi (less than 10 minutes from the end of your journey). The trip takes 1 hour 56 minutes to 2 hours 10 minutes, and the basic fare (excluding reservation charges) is ¥1,270.

Another possibility on the same line is the faster (usually by about 25 minutes) and more comfortable limited express (*tokkyū*, 特急), which has reserved seating, levies a ¥1,260 surcharge, and generally requires booking in advance. Limited expresses leave about twice an hour.

From the exit of Tōbu-Nikkō Station, turn right and traverse the pedestrian crossing a few meters on to Bus Stand No. 6 on the opposite side of the road. There, catch a Tōbu Bus bound for *Kirifuri-kōgen* (Kirifuri Highland, 霧降高原), and get off at the terminus. Bus times from late April to early November currently include 9:16, 9:48, 10:28, 11:31 A.M., and 1:31 P.M.. The approximately 25-minute journey takes you up a winding mountain road through attractive forest. The fare is ¥650.

From Kirifuri-kōgen to Ō Mountain (1 hour 15 minutes)

The bus ends up inside a large car park. At the left-hand side of this are steps leading up, signposted for the Lift Platform Entrance (リフト乗場入口). Go up these steps for a few minutes to another car park with views over the highland. Purple asters grow on the sides of the steps in summer. A short distance ahead to the left is a pedestrian tunnel, which you should follow to pass under the main road. Take the little walking path to the right, marked "Mountain Ascent Trail" (登山道), that leads off from the top of the first flight of stairs. This path runs through native forest and is fringed by *sasa* (dwarf bamboo). (Alternatively, continue up the stairs and catch the mountain lift up to the first station, which would save you a climb and about 15 minutes and, together with the slightly shorter ending to the trail described later, would reduce the rating of this walk to "E.")

The path emerges between the top of the first lift and a mountain hut-cum-restaurant. The views here are usually quite good, although when I visited it a swirling mist created an eerie atmosphere. It is possible to take the chairlifts higher to reach the area known as Kisuge Plain (*Kisuge-daira*, キスゲ平), where in summer the fields are carpeted with beautiful yellow *nikkōkisuge* (day lily, also known as *zenteika*). To continue the walk described here, go past the mountain hut to the bitumen lane and turn right, that is, downhill. Ignore the wide path to your left, which leads to Mts. Maru, Akanagi, and Nyohō (丸山 赤薙 女峰), and instead walk for about another 20 meters and turn right (before reaching the road and car park) along the equally wide trail signposted for Ō Mountain Hiking Course (大山ハイキングコース). This route is best known for its *mizunara* (oak) forest, and in late spring to early summer for its flowers of white *natsutsubaki* (camellia), orange *rengetsutsuji* (azalea), and white *zumi* (*Malus sieboldii*).

The early part of this trail, which is mostly descending, is a mecca for flora lovers, with flowering shrubs and numerous wildflowers, among them pink-white bunches of *fujibakama* (eupatorium thoroughwort or argueweed), small blue *tsuriganeninjin* (*Adenophora triphylla* var. *japonica*) bells, clumps of deep blue-purple *oyamarindō* (gentian), and various kinds of purple *azami* (thistle) in late summer. Hovering dragonflies are also plentiful. To protect this area, the sides of the trail are roped off.

In less than 10 minutes, the trail runs under the main road, and from here you simply follow the many signs for Ō Mountain (*Ō-yama*, 大山). The track descends quickly, passing through diverse forest with white hydrangealike flowering shrubs and offering good valley views in places. After 6 minutes or so, you cross a small bridge. Ignore the large but eventually impassable trail (道行不能) leading hard back to your right less than 10 minutes later. A further 4 minutes will see you scrambling through a rocky dale with a pretty stream (the upper reaches of the Kirifuri River), and a few minutes later you cross a smaller watercourse. In a number of places along this route, you will notice the track splits into two, but invariably these rejoin.

Subsequently, the trail runs through a gate and (via a ladder) over a fence—avoid the downhill path to the left—and then through a clearing as you begin to climb to the summit of Ō Mountain, soon visible in the distance. This slope also has a wealth of wildflowers: white-and-yellow chrysanthemums and others; and the strangely shaped, isolated trees on the right make an odd impression. You should reach the summit in about 30 minutes.

Around the little intersection of paths near the fence at the summit, appropriately marked "Top of Ō Mountain" (大山山頂), is a good lunch or rest stop, and the surrounding mountain views beyond the cleared fields of a nearby farm are appealing.

From Ō Mountain to Kirifuri-no-taki-iriguchi (1 hour 35 minutes)

To continue the walk, bear right in the direction of Tsutsuji Hill (*Tsutsuji-ga-oka*, ツツジケ丘 4.5 KM) and then head down the cleared slope, that is, do *not* follow the little ridge trail next to the barbed wire fence. At the time of writing, a detour to the left consisting of signs labeled "Temporary Hiking Course" (ハイキングコース 仮道) and black-and-yellow rope guides commenced about 50 meters down the slope. This detour takes you steeply down through native forest for about 10 minutes to a gravel road from the farm. Turn left there and follow the road downhill. When I walked this route, heavy rains had left this thoroughfare looking more like a riverbed.

About 5 minutes later, just beyond some gates, the walking track, signposted for Neko Flat (猫平), resumes to the left. This section of the trail ascends a cleared ridge, from which there are more views, and then makes its way down the other side. A *yamakagashi* (ring snake) shared part of this trail with me.

Some 10–15 minutes later, the track rejoins the road, only to depart to the left again about 50 meters on. Within a few minutes, you will arrive at Neko Flat (*Neko-no-daira*), where there is a choice of paths, both of which lead to Tsutsuji Hill. The route described here is the one to the right, toward Matsukura Waterfall and Tsutsuji Hill (マツクラ滝 ツツジケ丘 2.7 KM). This is perhaps a little more varied and serene than the alternative. The views from Neko Flat, which is dotted with pine trees, are also pleasing.

This way soon takes you over a fence and down a steep and

Morning dew greets the early hiker.

sometimes overgrown and slippery slope covered in *sasa* (dwarf bamboo). The trail splits and rejoins in a number of places. At the bottom of the slope after 10 minutes is a T-junction. To view Matsukura Waterfall, which is worth investigating, bear right as signposted (マツクラ滝 0.2 KM). Cross the road after a couple of minutes and climb the fence. Although it is difficult to get close to the waterfall, you can observe it best by crossing to the gravelly center bank of the river a few meters farther. Matsukura Waterfall (*Matsukura-no-taki*), which has quite a long drop, is up the tributary to the left (and not to be confused with the nearby, man-made rapid before the car bridge). There are also many wildflowers near the edge of the river, including mauve strings of *fujiutsugi* (buddleia), hanging pink *tsurifunesō* (snapweed or touch-me-not), and yellow *matsuyoigusa* (oenothera) in summer.

Return to the junction and proceed straight on, in the direction of Tsutsuji Hill (ツツジケ丘 2.3 KM). You will descend quickly and soon cross a fence, before shadowing the pretty Kirifuri River (marked on some maps as the Itaana River), which in places runs over a bed of whitish brown rock and down rapids. Equally attractive are the large orange *fushigurosennō* (*Lychnis miqueliana*) flowers that bloom here in summer. The trail subsequently winds through *sugi* (cedar) and *hinoki* (cypress) plantations with tall white crowns of *shishiudo* (*Angelica pubescens*) that in August emerge like bursts of fireworks from their ball-shaped buds. The path temporarily leaves the stream in order to negotiate a spur, passing a minor track on the way.

After approximately 20 minutes in forest with, in summer, pink-white-purple *yamaajisai* (hydrangea) and pink strands of winglike *nusubitohagi* (desmodium tickseed) flowers, and various frogs, the other trail from Neko Flat merges, but keep straight on, toward Tsutsuji Hill. Birds in the surrounding forest include *ōruri* (blue-and-white flycatcher), *kibitaki* (narcissus flycatcher), *uguisu* (bush warbler), *hototogisu* (little cuckoo), and *kakkō* (common cuckoo). Within a few minutes, you will come to the edge of the river. If the bridge that was washed out recently by heavy rains has not been replaced, follow the little-used track to the right upstream (next to the river bank) for about 50 meters and cross the river via the large fallen tree. On the other side, go left over the rocks, back downstream to where the trail resumes.

This rapidly leads you over a dry, rocky riverbed, and the continuation from there is marked by a sign for Tsutsuji Hill. The trail then rises out of the valley via log-and-earth steps and through a mix of native forest and *sugi* plantations with some white swirling blossoms of the *kōyabōki* (pertya) bush in summer. Ignore any trails leading off. About 10 minutes from the river, you should reach the top of a ridge, where the trail levels off and emerges beside the main road. (To reach the closest bus stop to the trail and thus shorten this walk by 10–15 minutes, go down to the road and continue on in the same direction.)

To complete the course described here, continue directly along the walking path, in the direction of Kirifuri Waterfall (霧降の滝), and in less than 10 minutes you reach a large car park in the vicinity of Tsutsuji Hill. Proceed straight through and follow the small road out past a children's playground. Beyond the restaurants, take the large road downhill to the right, past the tennis courts.

Purple *kobagibōshi* (hosta) and blue *akinotamurasō* (salvia) flowers grow on the sides of this road in summer. When you reach the main road after about 5 minutes, go straight, downhill. Kirifuri-no-taki-iriguchi (霧降の滝入口) Bus Stop is a short distance ahead on your left (last bus 4:31 P.M., ¥280). The trip back to Tōbu-Nikkō Station takes 7–10 minutes.

If you happen to have missed the last bus, you can walk back to the station in approximately 35 minutes. Just follow the main road downhill, and veer left to stay on it at the intersection after about 20 minutes. Impressive large yellow sheaths of *metakarakō* (ligularia) flourish on the right embankment in summer. Proceed straight through the traffic lights just before the long bridge over the Daiya River, and turn left at the lights on the other side. The station is then about 100 meters away on your left.

Another option, if you wish to stay overnight in the area and explore more the next day, is to stay in one of the numerous "pensions" on the road back to the station. One of these, Pension Kettle (tel. [0288] 54-0234, preferably in Japanese), is only 5 minutes or so downhill from Kirifuri-no-taki-iriguchi Bus Stop, and a shared room costs ¥8,800–¥9,800 (depending on the season) per person for one night (including two meals). Two youth hostels are located near Tōbu-Nikkō Station.

Return to Asakusa in Tokyo by following in reverse the instructions in the "Getting There" section for this walk.

14. LAKE CHŪZENJI

Course: Tōbu-Nikkō Station (by bus) → Ryūzu-no-taki Bus Stop → vicinity of Shōbu Beach → Aka Crag → Senju Beach → Tawara Rock → Bonji Crag → Shiro Crag → Point Matsu → Dainichi Point → Azegata → Uta Beach → Chūzenji Spa (by bus) → Tōbu-Nikkō Station

Reference map: Nitchi Map No. 30 (Okunikkō Okukinu, 奥日光 奥 鬼怒), Old Series No. 8; or Shōbunsha Map No. 31 (Nikkō, 日光), Old Series No. 43.

Walking time: About 4 hours 20 minutes.

Points of interest: An easy, if lengthy, walk around the attractive shore of Lake Chūzenji, clusters of wild azalea in spring and other flowers in summer, forest colors in autumn, Ryūzu and Kegon waterfalls.

GETTING THERE

At Asakusa Station (Platform 3 or 5), board a Tōbu Nikkō Line (東武日光線) rapid service train (*kaisoku*, 快速) bound for Tōbu-Nikkō (東武日光) Station. At the time of writing, such trains were leaving daily at 6:20, 7:10, 8:10, 9:10, and 10:20 A.M. As some separate at Shimo-Imaichi (下今市) Station, with the rear carriages going to Kinugawa (鬼怒川), be sure to board one of the front two carriages. Alight at the terminus. Seats can be reserved (for an additional ¥1,030) on the similar but less-frequent expresses (*kyūkō*, 急行), although you may have to change at Shimo-Imaichi (less than 10 minutes from the end of your journey). The trip takes 1 hour 56 minutes to 2 hours 10 minutes, and the basic fare (excluding reservation charges) is ¥1,270.

Another possibility on the same line is the faster (usually by about 25 minutes) and more comfortable limited express (*tokkyū*, 特急), which has reserved seating, levies a ¥1,260 surcharge, and generally requires booking in advance. Limited expresses leave about twice an hour.

From the exit of Tōbu-Nikkō Station, walk straight ahead to Bus Stand No. 1 and catch a Tōbu bus bound for Yumoto Onsen (湯元温泉). These leave every 30–40 minutes. Get off at Ryūzu-no-

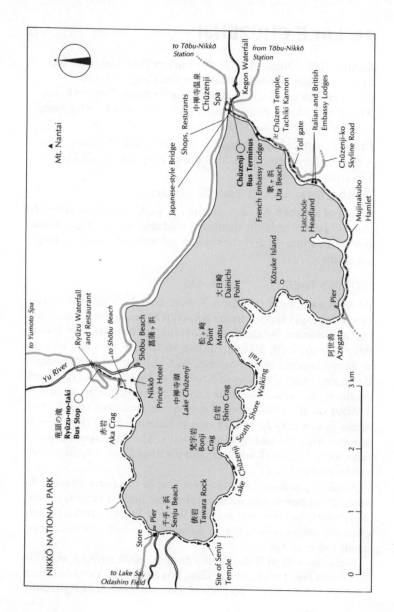

taki (竜頭の滝), after about 50 minutes. Early on in the ride, just after turning off the main road through Nikkō, you will see the sacred Shin Bridge (*Shinkyō*) over the Daiya River. You may spot monkeys along the way, especially when the bus is climbing up to Lake Chūzenji. The fare is ¥1,300.

From Ryūzu-no-taki to Senju Beach (1 hour)

Just a short distance back down the road from Ryūzu-no-taki Bus Stop and on the opposite side, a bitumen road leads uphill the 100 meters or so to Ryūzu Waterfall, after which the bus stop is named. This is a particularly impressive sight, and there is a beautifully sited restaurant there, so you may wish to visit it.

When you are ready, return to the bus stop and then take the lesser bitumen road that leads downhill to the left off the main road within a few meters. A sign in English indicates that this is the way to Nikkō Prince Hotel, and you will pass a number of company vacation houses and lodges. After about 4 minutes, a small dirt road flanking a dirt car park goes off to the right. Follow this road, which is signposted for Senju Beach (*Senju-ga-hama*, 千手ヶ浜). Within a few minutes, this road becomes a track that leads to a fork. In late summer, the fields surrounding this point are full of tall yellow *ōhangonsō* (rudbeckia goldenglow). Take the trail to the left, toward Senju Beach and Lake Sai (千手ヶ浜 西ノ湖). (This route actually runs behind Shōbu Beach, a popular camping area where the sightseeing vessels dock.)

You quickly enter forest and pass by a path to the left to Shōbu Beach (*Shōbu-ga-hama*, 菖蒲ヶ浜), but continue straight, in the direction of Senju Beach. The trail becomes a little rocky as you round a spur, and the sides of the trail are full of labeled trees native to these attractive woods: *azukinashi* (sorbus mountain ash), *hauchiwakaede* (maple), and *dakekanba* (a type of birch). In a few minutes, you will have your first views of Lake Chūzenji (*Chūzenji-ko*, 中禅寺湖) from high up on the path.

Twenty-one kilometers in circumference, the lake is quite large, and because of its relatively high altitude (about 1,200 meters) and consequent coolness, it is a resort popular in summer. Although yachting and fishing are the main draws, the mid-May cherry blossoms and brilliant autumn foliage are attractions that

Lake Chūzenji as seen from the start of the trail.

hikers especially can enjoy. The lake is also noted for its indigo blue color, though near the shore it takes on a greener hue, depending on the lighting. It was originally known in the Heian period (794–1185) as *Nan-ko* (South Lake), and in 1873 a local named Sadagoro Hoshino is supposed to have released some ten thousand fish into the lake, contributing to today's stocks of *ugui* (dace), *koi* (carp), and trout. The latter is represented by various kinds, including *nijimasu* (rainbow trout), *himemasu*, *honmasu*, and *buraunmasu*.

Wooden platforms assist you in the minor climb on this section, and various good lookout points are passed. Vines, as well as maples, *hinoki* (cypress), and *tōgokumitsubatsutsuji* (a pink-flowered azalea) are found along this path, which is a little up and down. In less than 15 minutes, you will arrive at Aka Crag (*Aka-iwa*, 赤岩), but continue on. Other labeled trees include *yogusominebari* (another kind of birch) and *ōkamenoki* (viburnum, which has white hydrangealike flowers in summer).

After approximately 6 minutes, this Nikkō National Park path leaves the side of the spur and descends into fairly flat, low forest with *mizunara* (oak). About 4 minutes later, you will pass by a clearing at the lake's edge, and from here on the trail mostly remains close to Lake Chūzenji's waters. This clearing could be a good lunch stop, as would many places along the entire length of this course. Some 10–15 minutes later you pass a hut and waterski ramp, and, after a further 10 minutes, the beach, store, picnic tables, and chairs at Senju Beach will appear immediately ahead.

Senju Beach is also a good rest area, if it isn't crowded. The views across the lake and to the dramatic 2,484-meter-high Mt. Nantai are particularly attractive, and the beach is good for walking and wading. There is also a pier from where boats leave for Shōbu Beach, Akegata, and Ōjiri near Chūzenji Spa (the latter two being a later destination and your approximate finish point, respectively). These could be used to shorten your walk, if desired, but note that the boats do not depart frequently, and then only between April and August. Fares range from about ¥400 to ¥600.

The dirt road off to the right—just before the store—is the way to Odashira Field (*Odashira-ga-hara*) and tiny Lake Sai (*Sai-no-ko*) (小田代ヶ原 西ノ湖), the latter a 30–40-minute walk. Odashira Field, like the adjacent *Senjō-ga-hara* (a walk through which is described in *Day Walks Near Tokyo*), is best known for its wonderful late spring/summer flowers. It is about 90 minutes away.

From Senju Beach to Azegata (2 hours 20 minutes)

To continue the trail described here, however, proceed along the dirt path parallel and close to the shore. This takes you past a campsite and various holiday houses on the right, and over a number of small bridges, ranging from little wooden structures over small streams to a suspension bridge crossing a river. In places boats are moored, and to your left Chūzenji Spa (*Chūzenji onsen*) can be seen on the far side of the lake. *Zumi* (*Malus sieboldii*) trees, which have prolific white blossoms in summer, are common here.

After one stretch of pebbled beach, the path rises a little to follow the undulating edge of the lake toward the east. This occurs 10–15 minutes from the Senju Beach store, and there is a wise warning (in English) on this section against attempting the walk during winter. (Inded, such a warning could well apply to any walks in the area in winter.) You will also go by the signposted site of former Senju Temple (千手堂). White summer daisies and *ōkamenoki* blossoms are other trailside attractions. Ignore the unmarked track to the right a few minutes later.

The beautiful native forest that follows has several concentrations of the springtime pink-flowered *shakunage* (azalea), readily identified by its clusters of curled leaves. *Mitsubatsutsuji* (another azalea with pink flowers in spring) also grows in the area. The trail bobs up and down a little—with nothing too strenuous—as it traces the lake's shoreline, which waterbirds often frequent. Because of the proximity to the water and the near-continuous shade of the vegetation, this route makes a good summer walk.

You will reach the point known as Tawara Rock (俵石) after 10–15 minutes. Continue along the rocky, rooty and, in places, slightly uphill trail that again makes use of wooden platforms to bridge difficult parts. The trail descends to open forest near the water, and in one place a sign points to Mt. Nantai (男体山), the spiritual symbol of Nikkō, across the lake. *Harigiri* (kalopanax) trees, recognizable by their needle-covered trunks, grow here, too. The rush of water you may hear is a small but swift stream that you cross before the path resumes its undulating pattern.

After about 25 minutes you will pass Bonji Crag (梵字岩), and there are signs along the way for Azegata (阿世潟), a later destination. A huge *katsura* (*Cercidiphyllum japonicum*) tree, patches of fungi, a stream, and several washed-away bridges are noticeable during the next 10–15 minutes, after which you arrive at the leftside turnoff to Shiro Crag Lookout (白岩展望台). It is worth going the very short distance along this path to its end, as it provides views of Shōbu Beach and Mt. Nantai.

Returning to the junction, turn left to proceed along the main path. Besides more *shakunage*, forest of *momi* (fir) and *mizunara* flourishes along this generally level section of the path, which incidentally is also known as the Lake Chūzenji South Shore Walking Trail (*Chūzenji-ko nangan hodō*, 中禅寺湖南岸歩道). You will cross more, mostly minor, bridges and streams, and the surface is at times very rocky. After about 35 minutes you will come to Point Matsu (*Matsu-ga-zaki*, 松ヶ崎), an area with brilliant crimson foliage in autumn, and 10–15 minutes later past many more *shakunage* to reach Dainichi Point (大日崎).

Another 15 minutes and you will notice a sign pointing to the left out toward tiny Kōzuke Island (*Kōzuke-jima*, 上野島), which is visible through the trees.

The final, 15–20 minute stretch to Azegata goes by a grave site and *noriutsugi* (white-flowered hydrangea) shrubs and *asunaro* (conifer) trees, and there are again distant vistas of Chūzenji Spa (*Chūzenji onsen*) across the lake. You will walk over bridges and through a clearing as you reach Azegata, which has campsites and a beach. Boats leave here for Ōjiri near Chūzenji Spa (but only infrequently, as previously mentioned).

From Azegata to Chūzenji Spa (1 hour)

Continue through the crisscross of paths and vehicle tracks of Azegata, keeping roughly parallel with and reasonably close to the water's edge. In a minute or two, you will reach a gravel road signposted for Tachiki Kannon (立木観音 3.4 KM). Veer left onto this road, which heads uphill past the pier, essentially following the shoreline (though a narrow headland known as *Hachōde-jima* is later bypassed).

This way leads you past a long beach, through forest with *sasa* (dwarf bamboo) and plenty of birds, including *kibitaki* (narcissus flycatcher), *ōruri* (blue-and-white flycatcher), *uguisu* (bush warbler), *tsugumi* (dusky thrush), and *komadori* (Japanese robin), and between numerous campsites popular with 4WD enthusiasts. Some 15–20 minutes later, you will walk through little Mujinakubo Hamlet. At this point, which has more summer *ōhangonsō*, the road surface becomes bitumen. Log cabins have been constructed here, and many boats line the long stony beach.

After perhaps 5–10 minutes, near a pier, the road winds uphill away from the water around a number of grand private summer houses, among them two belonging to the Italian and British embassies. In summer, blue-purple *torikabuto* (aconite or Japanese monkshood) flowers bloom in the vicinity.

Within 10 minutes, your road will pass the toll gate on the adjacent Chūzenji-ko Skyline road to your right, where little white clumps of *yamahahako* (anaphalis) flowers adorn the sides in

August. These two roads merge in a few minutes, but proceed straight on. Very shortly after, the waterfront promenade of the area known as *Uta-ga-hama* (Uta Beach, 歌ヶ浜) commences on your left. It is better to leave the road here and walk along the waterfront, where pleasant lake views, a pier, and usually a few hopeful fishermen add interest.

After a few minutes, when the promenade ends, go up the stone steps and follow the main road around to the left. Soon the elaborate entrance to Chūzen Temple (*Chūzen-ji*, 中禅寺) will become visible on your right. Inside this large complex is the tall Tachiki (literally, "living tree") Kannon, a very ancient wooden image of Kannon (the Goddess of Mercy), carved from a single Judas tree.

To complete the walk, keep going along the main road, past the French Embassy's villa, numerous lodgings and restaurants, and the ferry pier and boat hire area to the left. After crossing the Japanese-style bridge over a water channel (which carries water to Kegon Waterfall*), 15 minutes or so later, turn right at the T-junction and walk the few minutes to the bus terminus on your right. There catch any bus in the direction of Tōbu-Nikkō Station (*Tōbu-nikkō-eki*, 東武日光駅).

The bus trip takes 40–45 minutes and costs ¥1,050. Buses leave on average about every 30 minutes, with the last departing at approximately 8:30 P.M.. Note that the terminus of most buses is JR Nikkō Station, so make sure you get off at Tōbu-Nikkō Station, a few hundred meters before.

(*If you have time, you might consider visiting the spectacular 100-meter-high Kegon Waterfall [*Kegon-no-taki*, 華厳の滝] a few minutes away. One writer described Kegon as having "such a sheer descent that the wind and the air turn the water into a lace-like drapery, which, with the rising mist, gives the falls a peculiarly phantasmal beauty." The view from the top of the waterfall is particularly good, and an elevator whisks visitors to the bottom of the gorge. One less-appealing aspect of this natural wonder is that the falls are notorious for attracting numbers of potential suicides.)

Return to Asakusa Station in Tokyo by following in reverse the train instructions in the "Getting There" section for this walk.

15. THE TWIN LAKES OF KIRIKOMI AND KARIKOMI ——————— M

Course: Tōbu-Nikkō Station (by bus) → Kōtoku-iriguchi Bus Stop → Kōtoku Marsh → Kōtoku Farm → Sannō Pass → Kare Marsh → Lakes Kirikomi and Karikomi → Ko Pass → Yumoto Spa (by bus) → Tōbu-Nikkō Station

Reference map: Nitchi Map No. 30 (Okunikkō Okukinu, 奥日光奥鬼怒), Old Series No. 8; or Shōbunsha Map No. 31 (Nikkō, 日光), Old Series No. 43.

Walking time: About 3 hours 50 minutes.

Points of interest: Superb native forest, lakeside paths, alpine wildflowers, and sulfurous hot springs.

GETTING THERE

For this walk, it is recommended that you buy from the Tōbu ticket office at Asakusa Station (or any Tōbu Travel office) a Nikkō-Kinugawa Free Pass (日光鬼怒川フリーパス). This provides for travel by rapid service train from Asakusa to the Nikkō area and for unlimited travel on Tōbu buses within this area. The pass is good for 4 days, and costs ¥5,490.

At Asakusa Station (Platform 3 or 5), board a Tōbu Nikkō Line (東武日光線) rapid service train (*kaisoku*, 快速) bound for Tōbu-Nikkō (東武日光) Station. At the time of writing, such trains were leaving daily at 6:20, 7:10, 8:10, 9:10, and 10:20 A.M. As some separate at Shimo-Imaichi (下今市) Station, with the rear carriages going to Kinugawa (鬼怒川), be sure to board one of the front two carriages. Alight at the terminus. Seats can be reserved (for an additional ¥1,030) on the similar but less-frequent expresses (*kyūkō*, 急行), although you may have to change at Shimo-Imaichi (less than 10 minutes from the end of your journey). The trip takes 1 hour 56 minutes to 2 hours 10 minutes (and, for those without a Free Pass, costs ¥1,270, excluding reservation charges).

Another possibility on the same line is the faster (usually by about 25 minutes) and more comfortable limited express (*tokkyū*, 特急), which has reserved seating, levies a ¥1,260 surcharge, and

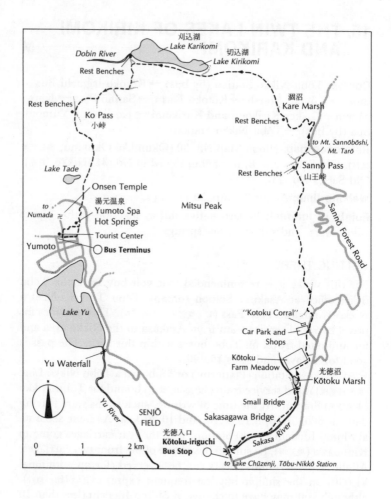

刈込湖
Lake Karikomi

Dobin River

切込湖
Lake Kirikomi

Rest Benches

涸沼
Kare Marsh

Rest Benches

Rest Benches

Ko Pass
小峠

to Mt. Sannōbōshi,
Mt. Tarō

Lake Tade

Rest Benches

Sannō Pass
山王峠

Onsen Temple

湯元温泉
Yumoto Spa
Hot Springs

to
Numada 卍

Mitsu Peak

Sannō Forest Road

Tourist Center

Yumoto

Bus Terminus

Lake Yu

"Kotoku Corral"

Car Park and
Shops

Kōtoku
Farm Meadow

光徳沼
Kōtoku Marsh

Yu Waterfall

Small Bridge

Sakasagawa Bridge

N

Yu River

SENJŌ
FIELD

光徳入口
Kōtoku-iriguchi
Bus Stop

Sakasa River

0   1   2 km

to Lake Chūzenji, Tōbu-Nikkō Station

generally requires booking in advance. Limited expresses leave about twice an hour.

From the exit of Tōbu-Nikkō Station, walk straight ahead to Bus Stand No. 1 and catch a Tōbu bus bound for Yumoto Onsen (湯元温泉). These leave every 30–40 minutes. Get off at Kōtoku-iriguchi (光徳入口), after about 1 hour. Early on in the ride, just after turning off the main road through Nikkō, you will see the sacred Shin Bridge (*Shinkyō*) over the Daiya River. You may spot monkeys along the way, especially when the bus is climbing up to Lake Chūzenji. The bus fare is ¥1,450 for those not holding a Free Pass.

From Kōtoku-iriguchi to Sannō Pass (1 hour 20 minutes)

From Kōtoku-iriguchi Bus Stop, walk in the direction the bus was traveling the short distance across Sakasagawa Bridge (*Sakasa-gawa-bashi*, 逆川橋). To the left is the area known as Senjō Field (*Senjō-ga-hara*, 戦場ヶ原), a walk through which is described in *Day Walks Near Tokyo*, and in summer beautiful pink *hozakishimotsuke* (*Spiraea salicifolia*) flowers bloom beside the road.

Just past the bridge, on the opposite side of the road, a trail begins to the right. Follow this path, marked "Sannō Pass and Kōtoku Farm" (山王峠 光徳牧場), which leads down near the often dry (at this point) stream bed and then along its left bank. The level trail shadows the pretty Sakasa River (*Sakasa-gawa*) through diverse native forest with birch trees, a number of shrubs that flower in summer, and various butterflies.

Within 20 minutes, you will reach a small bridge. Diverge right to cross this and then bear left toward Kōtoku (光徳). A few meters ahead is Kōtoku Marsh (*Kōtoku-numa*, 光徳沼), a delightful little pond with fish, tadpoles, and dragonflies, and a very picturesque mountain backdrop. Among the summer flowers found here are white *zumi* (*Malus sieboldii*, a kind of small apple tree), white clover, pink *hakusanfūro* (geranium cranesbill), and the many-headed white crowns of *shiraneninjin* (*Tilingia ajanensis*).

Proceed along the edge of the pond until you meet the fence of Kōtoku Farm (*Kōtoku bokujō*, 光徳牧場), where you should turn right. The meadow here usually contains horses and cows. At the corner of the meadow about 5 minutes from the pond and close to

Pretty Kōtoku Marsh.

a road, turn left, thus following the fence. Shortly after, veer right up the path with wooden handrails that leads to a car park, shops, and restaurants, and a picnic ground. Dairy products are sold here.

To reach the continuation of the trail, walk up the bitumen road beside the "KOTOKU CORRAL" store/restaurant, in the direction signposted (in English and Japanese) for Yumoto and Lakes Kirikomi and Karikomi (湯元 切込湖 刈込湖). Within 100 meters, bear left along the wide dirt path marked "Sannō Pass and Yumoto" (山王峠 湯元). Turn right in the similarly signposted direction soon after.

Again, there is diverse native forest, here with the added attraction in summer of the occasional bright orange *kurumayuri*, a large, wheel-shaped lily. Avoid the wide, unmarked path to the right after a few minutes, and shortly after, where cars must stop, veer left away from the little stream.

From this point, the trail begins to ascend, often by means of steps, through diverse forest of *mizunara* (oak) and birch, often with *sasa* (dwarf bamboo) undergrowth that is home to many birds. (This area is particularly popular with birdwatchers.) The mountain on your left is Mitsu Peak (*Mitsu-dake*, 三岳).

You should reach the rest benches near Sannō Pass (*Sannō-tōge*, 山王峠) about 50 minutes after leaving the car park. This is a good place for lunch, although the best views are found a little farther on.

From Sannō Pass to Yumoto Onsen (2 hours 30 minutes)

From the intersection of trails beside the benches near Sannō Pass, veer right in the direction labeled "Kare Marsh and Yumoto" (涸沼 湯元). The level trail through the pass offers good views of the forested slopes. Ignore the minor paths that descend to the left. Keep left, toward Kare Marsh and Yumoto, at the signposted fork a few minutes from the rest benches. (The overgrown track to the right leads to Mt. Sannōbōshi and Mt. Tarō [山王帽子山 太郎山], the two nearby peaks to your right.) A minute or two later, the trail passes close to Sannō Forest Road, before descending steeply. Parts of the path are paved with cobblestones, and it is possible to see right across the valley. You will arrive at the bottom, where Kare Marsh (*Kare-numa*, 涸沼) lies, in about 20 minutes.

Kare Marsh is actually a dry, grassy bowl surrounded by high mountains, and in summer it is a botanist's delight, a giant untended garden of alpine and other wildflowers. Beautiful purple *ayame* (iris), cone-shaped arrays of tiny mauve *tegatachidori* orchids, pink *hakusanchidori* orchids, yellow *yamaodamaki* (aquilegia columbine), white *karamatsusō* (feather columbine), pink *yanagiran* (willow herb), white brushes of *kobaikeisō* lilies, and even pink *tsutsuji* (azalea) are just some of these. In one place, rest benches command a view of the entire marsh.

The trail climbs out the other side of the valley, through a rocky, *sasa*-covered gap between peaks, and levels off after about 15 minutes. From there, it follows a reasonably flat path through native forest. Isolated but spectacular outcrops of yellow, orange, and other-colored fungi and mushrooms decorate this pretty landscape.

In 15 minutes or so, you should have your first view (to the right) of Lake Kirikomi (*Kirikomi-ko*, 切込湖), an attractive body of green water surrounded by dense woods. The path runs above the southern shore, but does not actually descend to the water's edge. Later, you will see that the lake narrows, before opening out into its larger sister, Lake Karikomi (*Karikomi-ko*, 刈込湖). The lakes were formed when lava from the volcanic Mitsu Peak blocked the flow of water. The surrounding forest is composed of *kometsuga* (Japanese hemlock), *tōhi* (Japanese spruce), *shirabe* (fir), and *asunaro* (cypress).

Some 20–25 minutes later, you will reach an intersection near the western end of Lake Karikomi. The path to Yumoto continues straight on and then up to the left, in the direction marked for Ko Pass and Yumoto (小峠 湯元), but if you have time, take the track to the right, which leads the short distance down to a small beach on the edge of the lake. This pleasant spot has rest benches and is frequented by wild ducks. The Dobin River (*Dobin-zawa*, ドビン沢) flows into the lake near this place.

Returning to the nearby intersection, walk uphill in the direction of Ko Pass and Yumoto. This track through rocky, ferny forest leads steeply up for 15–20 minutes to a T-junction, where you should turn right onto the wide path, also signposted for Ko Pass and Yumoto. The path runs level, turns right to descend steeply, and then levels off again before reaching Ko Pass (*Ko-tōge*, 小峠) approximately 15 minutes later. Rest benches have been erected on one side.

From the pass, go straight ahead, in the direction labeled for Yumoto and Yu Waterfall (湯元 湯滝), or just Yumoto (湯元). This section also has cobblestone paving (which can be slippery) in its initially steep descent, but the incline soon becomes gentler. Occasionally, there are views of Lake Yu (*Yu-no-ko*, 湯ノ湖) in the distance, and the smell of the sulfurous waters of Yumoto Spa (*Yumoto onsen*, 湯元温泉) grows stronger as you proceed.

After 25 minutes, cross over the main road and walk down the steps on the other side. In less than 10 minutes, you will reach the hot springs, most of which have covers, at the bottom of the slope. The water is a very pleasant temperature. Continue along the gravel trail past these to a junction where a path comes in from the right. To reach Yumoto Onsen Bus Terminus, a short distance away, two possibilities exist. You can walk straight ahead the short distance to the bitumen road, where you should turn right. Go past the various inns for about 100 meters to the bus terminus, which is on the left. Alternatively, from the junction, bear right across the wooden platform through the marsh, in the direction of Onsen Temple (*Onsen-ji*, 温泉寺). This is an interesting route, as the marsh has frogs, *susuki* (pampas grass), and wildflowers in summer. The temple boasts a belltower, but the structure is new and of little interest (though the main building does contain a very old image of Yakushi Nyorai, the Buddha of Healing). When you reach the gravel road, turn left. Walk 100 meters straight on to the bitumen road. The bus terminus lies a little farther on, to the right.

A number of restaurants are grouped near the bus terminus. Accommodation in the area is heavily booked in summer, and charges are about ¥10,000 per person, although the Tourist Center (*Kankō Sentā*, 観光センター) behind the terminus sometimes has cheaper lodgings. Reasonably priced accommodation is more readily found around Chūzenji Spa (中禅寺温泉) near the eastern end of Lake Chūzenji (*Chūzenji-ko*). Sugimoto-kan (すぎもと館, tel. [0288] 55-0161 in Japanese) lies about 50 meters from Chūzenji's main bus station and offers Japanese-style accommodation and two meals for about ¥5,700 per person. The two Youth Hostels in the vicinity of Tōbu-Nikkō Station also provide a cheaper alternative.

Buses for Tōbu-Nikkō Station leave from Bus Stand No. 1. The trip takes approximately 1 hour 10 minutes (and costs ¥1,600 if you don't have a Free Pass).

16. THE GANMAN POOLS ──────── D

Course: Tōbu-Nikkō Station → Tennō-san Shrine → Mt. Kō-no-su → Mt. Nakimushi → Ga Peak → Doppyō → The Ganman Pools → Sōgō-kaikan-mae Bus Stop (by bus) → Tōbu-Nikkō Station

Reference map: Nitchi Map No. 30 (Okunikkō Okukinu, 奥日光奥鬼怒), Old Series No. 8; or Shōbunsha Map No. 31 (Nikkō, 日光), Old Series No. 43.

Walking time: About 4 hours.

Points of interest: Views of Nikkō City and surrounding ranges, spring and summer wildflowers, the stunning Ganman Pools area of the Daiya River, and Nikkō's historical monuments (additional walking).

Note: Insect spray is useful in summer, as mosquitoes are plentiful on some parts of this trail. Also, if you intend to visit the nearby religious monuments after the walk, you might consider obtaining in advance a guide to these structures and their fascinating history from Tokyo's Tourist Information Center.

GETTING THERE

At Asakusa Station (Platform 3 or 5), board a Tōbu Nikkō Line (東武日光線) rapid service train (*kaisoku*, 快速) bound for Tōbu-Nikkō (東武日光) Station. At the time of writing, such trains were leaving daily at 6:20, 7:10, 8:10, 9:10, and 10:20 A.M. As some separate at Shimo-Imaichi (下今市) Station, with the rear carriages going to Kinugawa (鬼怒川), be sure to board one of the front two carriages. Alight at the terminus. Seats can be reserved (for an additional ¥1,030) on the similar but less-frequent expresses (*kyūkō*, 急行), although you may have to change at Shimo-Imaichi (less than 10 minutes from the end of your journey). The trip takes 1 hour 56 minutes to 2 hours 10 minutes, and the basic fare (excluding reservation charges) is ¥1,270.

Another possibility on the same line is the faster (usually by about 25 minutes) and more comfortable limited express (*tokkyū*, 特急), which has reserved seating, levies a ¥1,260 surcharge, and generally requires booking in advance. Limited expresses leave about twice an hour.

From Tōbu-Nikkō Station to Mt. Kō-no-su (55 minutes)

From the exit of Tōbu-Nikkō Station, walk straight out past the bus stands, cross the main road, and then proceed down the road almost directly ahead (to the left of the red Post Office box). In front of you, a large Lion Do Supermarket should be visible a few blocks away. Go toward the supermarket, but turn right just before the Shidobuchi River and Shidobuchi Bridge (しどぶちばし), a few minutes from the station. Follow this lane, which runs to the east of the station beside a tributary of the large Daiya River, the banks of which have many wildflowers. Local people cultivate the riverbed in places.

This way leads you past a historical board and a hiking course sign marked "To Mt. Nakimushi via Mt. Tennō" (天王山を圣て 鳴虫山に至る). The historical board shows the approximate position of a number of interesting sites, including a memorial tower for the souls of those who died when the nearby Inari River flooded in the second year of the Kanbun era (1662), and the grave of a shogunate army spy caught and executed by the Imperial Army during an early morning battle on April 5, the fourth year of the Keiō era (1868).

At the crossroads just after a nursery school, 10–15 minutes from your previous turn, bear left across the green steel bridge. On the other side, and a little farther on, are signs for "Access to Mt. Nakimushi" (鳴虫山登山口). Follow this lane straight ahead, uphill. Its surface becomes gravel as it curves around to the right. Within a couple of minutes you will see a mapboard and concrete steps to your left. Climb these steps, swing right, and follow the gravel path next to the fence. This steep trail zigzags up a slope that has white hydrangea in summer and orange *yamatsutsuji* (azalea) blossoms in spring.

In about 7 minutes, turn right at the T-junction and walk through the *torii* (shrine gateway) to tiny Tennō-san Shrine (*Tennō-san-jinja*, 天王山神社). Besides being a pleasant rest spot with good views of Nikkō City, this area has many summer wildflowers: white wild roses, purple cobs of *utsubogusa* (prunella

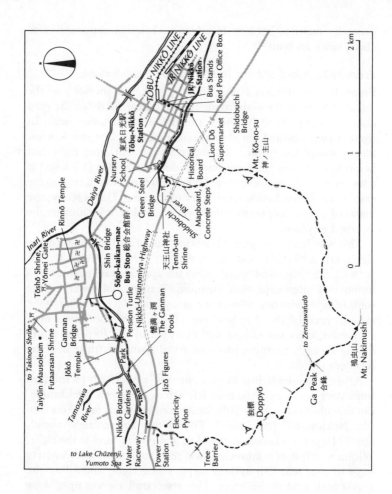

self-heal), and at least one kind of the queerly shaped, yellow-green *tōdaigusa* (euphorbia). Maple and cherry trees also grow here.

When you are ready, return to the junction and continue straight on, uphill through the conifer forest. Ignore the unmarked track leading hard back to the left a few minutes later, and keep left (virtually straight on) at the fork signposted for Mt. Kō-no-su and Mt. Nakimushi (神ノ主山 鳴虫山) after about 2 more minutes.

This rocky, rooty trail passes through a mix of natural and planted forest, and the former attracts a number of avian residents and visitors. *Sasa* (dwarf bamboo) flourishes in places along the path sides. Turn right at the T-junction some 15 minutes later, again toward Mt. Nakimushi (鳴虫山). Fluffy pink clusters of *shimotsuke* (spiraea) decorate the trail edges here in July.

The vistas back toward Nikkō City open out as you climb higher, and after approximately 7 minutes you will arrive at the summit of Mt. Kō-no-su (*Kō-no-su-yama*), where benches afford a comfortable stop. Extensive panoramas and the many summer long white cones of *okatoranoo* (chlethra loosestrife) and beautiful purple *ayame* (iris) blooms make this a pretty location.

From Mt. Kō-no-su to Ga Peak (1 hour 20 minutes)

As you continue down the other side of Mt. Kō-no-su, raspberries and dragonflies are pleasant distractions in summer, but the flies can be annoying. The path traverses a level ridge with mixed conifer and native forest, before heading steeply up. (Although the track briefly divides into two—both here and at various places later—the branches soon rejoin.) In fact, this whole section consists essentially of a series of steepish climbs, punctuated by level stretches of ridge—with even the occasional minor descent—as you make your way toward Mt. Nakimushi.

Fine clusters of mauve *koajisai* (*Hydrangea hirta*) flowers in summer, and in springtime exotic mauve *katakuri* (dogtooth violet or adder's tongue lily) and various other kinds of azalea—pink *akayashio*, white *shiroyashio*, and pink *tōgokumitsubatsutsuji*—dominate until the summit of Mt. Nakimushi. There are also some large *buna* (Japanese beech) trees and occasional mountain views along the way. Keep on the main path at the small peak after 40–45 minutes.

You should reach the 1,104-meter-high top of Mt. Nakimushi (*Nakimushi-yama*) about 17 minutes later. Although this is the highest peak on this trail, the view is limited by the vegetation. Locals say that when there's mist on Mt. Nakimushi, it is going to rain.

To proceed, go right at the T-junction at the summit, in the direction of the Ganman Pools (憾満ヶ渕, a derivation from the original name of "Kanman" and marked on some signs as 合満ヶ渕 or even 合満ヶ淵). The rocky path descends steeply via log-and-earth steps into attractive native forest with more azaleas.

Again the *sasa*-bordered path runs up and down via ridges between peaks, and in one place it becomes quite narrow and a little overgrown. After about 20 minutes, you will arrive at Ga Peak (*Gappō*, written as either 合峰 or 合方, depending on the signpost, and also marked on some maps as 松立山). Long ago, the area was a place of pilgrimage for priests. Just 20 meters lower than Mt. Nakimushi, this peak also offers excellent vistas if the weather and summer growth permits. In favorable conditions, Nikkō's major mountains and landmarks, including Mts. Nantai (男体山), Ōmanago (大真名子山), Komanago (小真名子山), Taishaku (帝釈山), Nyohō (女峰山), and Akanagi (赤薙山), and Ichiri-ga-sone (一里が曽根), as well as Kirifuri Highland (霧降高原, described in another walk in this guide), are visible.

From Ga Peak to Sōgō-kaikan-mae (1 hour 45 minutes)

Resume the walk by taking the path almost immediately ahead, again toward the Ganman Pools. (The path to the right leads to Zenizawafudō [銭沢不動].) Steps also assist you down this steep slope, and the path undulates, as previously, with more good views. Notable flora here ranges from summer daisies, yellow beads of *kokinreika* (patrina), spidery white *karamatsusō* (feather columbine), and raspberries (as well as other wildflowers already mentioned) to ferns. There are also many white-flowered Japanese hydrangeas from this point on, and the forest fluctuates between mixed and plantation, with some pine trees. As before, the path splits into two in various places, but these soon converge.

The swirling pools and rapids of the Daiya River's *Ganman-ga-fuchi*.

After about 45 minutes, you will reach the top of the small, probably unmarked peak known as Doppyō (独標). Keep to the right at the fork there—this track, too, descends steeply and is slippery in places.

At the junction 20–25 minutes later, bear right (the path straight on is blocked off by a tree barrier) in the direction of the Ganman Pools. You can see a road and part of the town from here. After continuing downward fairly precipitously, mostly through plantations, the trail levels off in dense undergrowth and within 15 minutes becomes a vehicle track. Ignore the track soon after to the left. In a few minutes, this way winds around an electricity pylon and passes a hydroelectric station and a gate (again ignore a track to the left) and then under the Nikkō-Utsunomiya Highway. Swing right onto the bitumen road just beyond this.

A short distance on, follow the walking path, signposted for the Ganman Pools (*Ganman-ga-fuchi*, 憾満ヶ淵), that leads off to the left. You can see a water raceway (from the nearby power station) that runs into the river on your left. On the right there soon begins a long line of old and beautiful stone Jizō (the guardian deity of children and travelers) figures on pedestals (known as the "Bake Jizō," 化地蔵), numbering perhaps one hundred, a surviving tribute to their carvers' skill. Within a few minutes to the left are a series of stunning waterfalls, rapids, and swirling pools fed by an aqua-colored flow—the natural wonder named the Ganman Pools. A small wooden shelter provides shade for spectators, but the fishermen cast from the rocks. In summer, bushes of white-and-purple *tamaajisai* (another kind of Japanese hydrangea) complete this seemingly perfect scene. Photography enthusiasts will find this sacred place a good subject.

Subsequently, the trail leads out of an entrance gate and through a long park and past a gateball (a version of croquet) field, before rejoining the road after about 5 minutes. A number of historical sites dot this area. Go left along the road and across the Ganman Bridge (*Ganman-bashi*) over the Daiya River (*Daiya-gawa*).

In about 5 minutes, you will see Pension Turtle on the right, within that part of Nikkō City called Takumi-chō. This is an excellent place to stop for the night, if you have the time and would like to see more of Nikkō the following day. A good location, friendly staff, and appetizing food are some of the pension's assets. The cost of rooms for two persons starts from about ¥7,600 (both Japanese- and Western-style accommodation are available), and meals are extra. Bookings are a must (tel. [0288] 53-3168, in English or Japanese.)

Walk on, turn right at the T-junction, then left shortly after, then right at the next T-junction as you go up the hill. When you reach the main road some 5–10 minutes after the pension, you should cross over the road and go to the left, if you wish to return immediately to Tōbu-Nikkō Station. You can do this via the pedestrian underground passages below the intersection. Sōgō-kaikan-mae (総合会館前) Bus Stop is just a few meters up the road. The ¥210 journey to the station only takes about 5 minutes, and buses run until quite late.

Alternatively, you could walk back to Tōbu-Nikkō Station, which requires 25–30 minutes. To do this, turn right rather than left at the main road, and when you reach the intersection after the sacred Shin Bridge (*Shinkyō*), turn right across the Daiya River. This way leads you down the main street of Nikkō City, with its many restaurants and souvenir shops. The station is on your left.

Another alternative if you have time before heading back to Tokyo is to take a look at some of Nikkō's exemplary temples and shrines, which are quite close to this intersection. Follow the signs in English in the pedestrian underground passage to get to the temple named *Rinnō-ji*, and other major attractions. Tōshō Shrine (*Tōshō-gū*), dedicated to Ieyasu Tokugawa, the founder of the Tokugawa Shogunate, with its elaborately carved Yōmei Gate (*Yōmei-mon*), said to hypnotize admirers and make them watch it until twilight, and the ornate Taiyūin Mausoleum (*Taiyūin-reibyō*), the shrine venerating the third Tokugawa Shōgun, Iemitsu, are just a few of the numerous and well-signposted historical monuments in the vicinity.

To return to Tokyo's Asakusa Station from Tōbu-Nikkō Station, follow in reverse the train instructions in the "Getting There" section for this walk.

IBARAKI-CHIBA

The vast Ibaraki and Chiba prefectures run in a giant arc from the northeast to the southeast of Tokyo. Although they are relatively flat—resulting in dense population centers, with much of the remaining land being farmed—there still remain some excellent areas for walking, with a wide range of difficulty. These are to be found on Chiba's beautiful Bōsō Peninsula, in the more rugged northwestern part of Ibaraki, and in other isolated pockets. Of interest on these walks are the local fauna and historical sites, as well as sea views, fine forests, and a host of wildflowers. Numerous railways (especially the Keisei Line from Ueno, the Uchibō and Sotobō lines out of Tokyo and connecting lines in Chiba, and the Jōban and Tōhoku main lines leaving from Ueno and linking railways in Ibaraki) and a network of buses provide excellent access.

17. BŌSŌ'S ANCIENT MOUNDS ——— E

Course: Shimousa-Manzaki Station → Sakata Pond → Bōsō's Ancient Mounds → [Museum → Burial Mounds → Aquatic Botanical Gardens → Ryūkaku Temple → Museum → Bōsō Village] → Sakata Pond → Shimousa-Manzaki Station

Reference map: Narita (成田) 1:25,000 Sheet Map.

Walking time: 1 hour 40 minutes, depending on how many sites are visited, plus sightseeing time. (There are sufficient attractions for a very full day.)

Points of interest: A flattish, easy trail suitable for families with children, numerous burial mounds and an associated museum with relics dating back to the fourth century, extremely diverse forest and a wide range of wildflowers, water- and other birds, and Bōsō Village (a collection of reconstructed shops and houses from Edo times).

GETTING THERE

From JR Ueno Station, it is best to take a Narita (成田)-bound rapid service train (*kaisoku*, 快速) on the JR Narita Line (成田線), and alight at Shimousa-Manzaki (下総松崎) after 1 hour 9–14 minutes. Currently, these trains leave only at 7:17, 7:45, and 8:55 A.M. Check the electronic train information board at Ueno Station for the platform number.

Alternatively, take any Jōban Line (常磐線) local (*futsū*, 普通) train from Ueno Station (Platform 10, 16, 17, or 18, depending on the time) to Abiko (我孫子) Station (30–38 minutes). At Abiko, transfer to a Narita-bound train for the remaining 33–40 minutes and get off at Shimousa-Manzaki Station. These trains leave about twice an hour.

Regardless of which of these two possibilities you use, the fare will be ¥880. Note that some Chiyoda Line trains of the Tokyo subway system also terminate at Abiko.

From Shimousa-Manzaki to Bōsō's Ancient Mounds Museum
(40 minutes)

Leave Shimousa-Manzaki Station by its only exit, and take the little bitumen lane to the left, parallel with the tracks. Two Kantō Community Path (*Kantō-fureai-no-michi*, 関東ふれあいの道) signs (recognizable by their green leaf emblems) indicate that this is the way to Bōsō's Ancient Mounds (*Bōsō-fūdoki-no-oka*, 房総風土記の丘 2.5 km) and Jinbei Ferry (*Jinbei-watashi*, 甚兵衛渡し).

Within a few minutes, you will reach a T-junction, where you should turn right toward Bōsō's Ancient Mounds. (The road to the left, across the railway line, leads to Jinbei Ferry.) In summer, the field to your left has bright pink *ōinutade* (polygonum) and white balls of *seri* (dropwort or Japanese parsley) flowers. After one more minute, turn left, then almost immediately right, at the signposted junctions. This larger road has paddy fields to the right and, in summer, yellow *matsuyoigusa* (oenothera primrose) wildflowers along its edges, particularly on the left. In groves in the area stand *tabunoki* (*Machilus thunbergii*), *shirakashi* (a type of oak), *sugi* (cedar), *keyaki* (zelkova), *take* (bamboo), and *sudajii* (*Castanopsis cuspidata* var. *sieboldii*).

After about 10 minutes, on the other side of a small rise, you will see a lesser, signposted road to the left. Follow this road toward Bōsō's Ancient Mounds (until you reach these burial

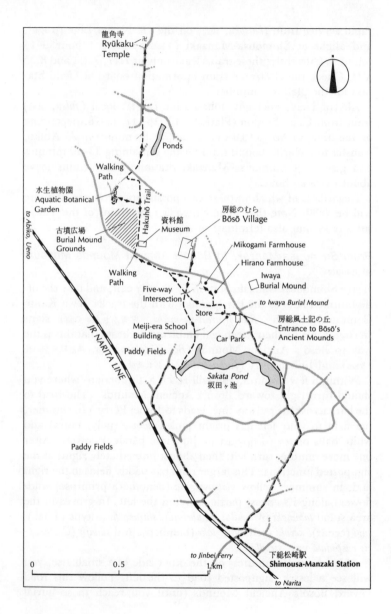

龍角寺
Ryūkaku
Temple

Ponds

Walking
Path

水生植物園
Aquatic Botanical
Garden

Hakuhō Trail

古墳広場
Burial Mound
Grounds

資料館
Museum

房総のむら
Bōsō Village

Mikogami Farmhouse

Hirano Farmhouse

Iwaya
Burial Mound

Walking
Path

Five-way
Intersection

to Iwaya Burial Mound

Store

Meiji-era School
Building

Car Park

房総風土記の丘
Entrance to Bōsō's
Ancient Mounds

to Abiko, Ueno

JR NARITA LINE

Paddy Fields

Sakata Pond
坂田ヶ池

Paddy Fields

to Jinbei Ferry

下総松崎駅
Shimousa-Manzaki Station

to Narita

0   0.5   1 km

mounds, ignore signs that do not belong to the Kantō Community Path system), to a fork just a few minutes on, where you should go right, as indicated by the sign.

Almost immediately, the eastern end of Sakata Pond (*Sakata-ga-ike*, 坂田ヶ池) will be visible to the left. The pond is the result of damming, and is surrounded by groves of trees. Most of the waterplants you can see at the surface are *himegama* rushes. A few old wooden punts are moored here, and waterfowl, grebes, and kingfishers may be seen.

Continue by following the edge of the pond for a couple of minutes around to the road (or take the small gravel lane that runs nearby) and then go left. This road winds up a small hill past vegetable fields and greenhouses on the left. Various summer wildflowers, including purple clover, *takatōdai* (euphorbia), and the spectacular giant *yamayuri* (gold-banded lily, the first of many adorning the sides of this trail) dot the roadside.

In about 7 minutes, on the left you will arrive at the entrance to Bōsō's Ancient Mounds and its large car park. (Admission to this, and indeed all attractions described for this walk, is free.) To the right, on the other side of the road and less than 5 minutes away, is Iwaya Burial Mound (*Iwaya-kofun*, 岩屋古墳), the largest of the Ryūkakuji group of 113 tumuli (ancient tombs in the form of ar-tificial mounds). This designated national treasure measures 78 meters along its square sides and is 13 meters high. Follow the marked trail to reach it.

Around Bōsō's Ancient Mounds (70 minutes, excluding viewing times)

Proceeding from the entrance of Bōsō's Ancient Mounds, walk down the wide promenade, past the car park, toward a store sell-ing refreshments. To the left is the restored Meiji-period auditorium of an elementary school, Gakushūin, constructed in Tokyo in 1899. The different trees around the building are the symbols of various towns and cities in the Chiba area and are labeled with their species and family.

At the store, turn right, in the direction of the old Hirano and Mikogami residences (旧平野家住宅 旧御子神家住宅). This lovely wide track through diverse forest, containing to the east groves of *akamatsu* (red pine), *kunugi* (oak), and *konara* (another kind of oak), leads in less than 5 minutes to a junction with a road leading to the right. Turn right there, toward the old Hirano and Mikogami farmhouses. The surrounding trees are all labeled in *kana* (the Japanese phonetic scripts), and a wealth of wildflowers flourishes among the ground cover. *Enaga* (long-tailed tit), *mejiro* (Japanese white-eye), and *shijūkara* (great tit) live in these woods.

The first of the two grand old renovated farmhouses you reach after a minute or so belonged to the Hirano family and was erected in 1751. The former Mikogami family residence (1779) is a similar distance farther on. Both thatched houses contain old furniture, implements, and clothing, and exhibit skilled construction techniques that took advantage of the natural shapes of trees, especially in roof joists.

Return to the junction and proceed right, in the direction of the museum and the main burial mound grounds (資料館 古墳広場). Many small tumuli (with green signs giving their identification numbers and dimensions) flank the way. In a few minutes, after passing through a bamboo grove, you will reach a five-way junction. To the left is the return path (the final part of your walk) to Shimousa-Manzaki Station (下総松崎駅). Ahead and to the right are paths to the museum and main burial mound grounds, while hard right and back is another track to the farmhouses you have just visited. Continue straight ahead, toward the museum and burial grounds. In about 4 minutes, the trail joins another walking path that runs parallel with a bitumen road. Bear left onto this path and in 2 minutes you will see a new museum building on your right across the road. (A walking track [遊歩道] commences to the left.)

This museum houses a well-arranged collection of objects both natural and man-made from the Chiba area, with a number of identifying labels in English, but many of the items are self-explanatory. The lower floor is dedicated to displays associated with burial mounds and ancient temples in the Bōsō area and includes *haniwa* (clay images), bronze mirrors, and weapons from the tumuli (dating back to at least the fourth century), as well as relics from nearby Ryūkaku Temple. Upstairs are fossils of marine creatures that lived when Chiba was still under the sea, and a reconstruction of the Naumann elephant bones found in Inba

Marsh, also nearby. Archaeological remains from the stone age through the Jōmon, Yayoi, and later periods are also on display. Outside the museum are two stone constructions illustrating the position of the deceased in the tombs, and the overall layout of the tombs is shown in drawings inside the museum. The museum is open from 9:00 A.M. to 4:30 P.M. every day except Mondays.

Just beyond the museum, on the same side of the road, are the main burial grounds, a wide, grassy parklike area with numerous large tumuli. A shady spot here would be ideal for a picnic.

Between the burial grounds and the museum is a gravel path, part of an ancient trail known as the *Hakuhō-dō* (白鳳道), which you should follow if you wish to visit either the small Aquatic Botanical Garden or Ryūkaku Temple. The trail encountered to the left after about 3 minutes, marked "水生植物園," leads the short distance to the Aquatic Botanical Garden. (Straight on is the route to Ryūkaku Temple [龍角寺].) To reach the garden, you will have to leave this trail after just a few minutes and descend to your right. There are several ponds with various waterplants, among them *mitsugashiwa* (bogbean or marsh trefoil) and irises, and between two of the ponds is a rest house next to a small bridge. (The main track you departed from continues on and could be used to return eventually to the museum.)

To walk to Ryūkaku Temple, return to the junction and head left in the direction signposted for that place (龍角寺). After a minute, the trail brushes the edge of a highway and then descends to run beneath this road. Ignore any trails diverging (some to the right head down to another pond). You pass a small shrine and then go between vegetable fields before joining a gravel vehicle track—walk straight ahead. A few minutes on, at the intersection of bitumen roads, continue straight through in the signposted direction, along the bitumen road. Ryūkaku Temple (*Ryūkaku-ji*) is less than 4 minutes away on the left side, at a slight curve in the road.

The temple is one of the oldest Buddhist places of worship in eastern Japan, and its origin is believed to be related to a powerful family that controlled the area in the seventh century. Some ancient elements can be found in the grounds, but most of the con-

A twelfth-century Buddha head in
Bōsō-fūdoki-no-oka's museum.

structions are fairly new. The temple grounds seem to have more than their share of tunnel-digging *mogura* (moles).

Return to the museum and follow to the left (back in the direction you originally arrived from) the dirt roadside path on the other side of the road. When, after 5 minutes, you reach an intersection with a sign pointing to the left to Bōsō Village (*Bōsō-no-mura*, 房総のむら), obey this sign and cross the road. Walk along the wide gravel path for 2 minutes to this attraction's entrance on the left side.

Bōsō Village is an absorbing collection of reconstructions of old Bōsō area shops and structures from late Edo to early Meiji period. These include establishments making and selling noodles, kimono, confectioneries, books, paper, crafts, liquor, medicines, fish, chinaware, women's accessories, tea, as well as tatami, woodworking and blacksmith shops, with a main street re-creating old Sawara and other Chiba towns. There is also a farmhouse, a *ryokan* (traditional Japanese inn), and a samurai's residence. The attraction of this interactive museum is that visitors may make arrangements (at the information counter) to try their hand at the various crafts. Folk and martial arts are also presented during the year, and English-language pamphlets are available at the gate.

From Bōsō's Ancient Mounds to Shimousa-Manzaki Station (30 minutes)

To return to Shimousa-Manzaki Station, from Bōsō Village go back to the road, cross it and continue straight for a couple of minutes until you arrive back at the five-way intersection. There, proceed straight ahead toward the station, as signposted (下総松崎駅). The forest to the west has in places *azumanezasa* (a thin kind of bamboo), *shirodamo* (*Neolitsea sericea*), *akagashi* (evergreen oak), and *hisakaki* (*Eurya japonica*). Ignore any paths leading off, and in about 5 minutes you will pass by the western end of Sakata Pond. Turn right up the concrete path at the end of the pond, and then left a minute later onto the small bitumen road. To the right paddy fields stretch into the distance, and you can make out part of the northern arm of the lake known as Inba Marsh (*Inba-numa*, 印旛沼, a walk around whose western extent is described in *Day Walks Near Tokyo*).

Ignore the small roads to the right, but veer right downhill when the road forks after 3–4 minutes. I found delicate mauve *himeyaburan* (*Liriope minor*, a tiny relative of the lily family) along the left side of this lane. About 5 minutes later, a T-junction forces you to make a choice—go right, then left after 50 meters or so, along a main road. Some 4 minutes later you will be back at an intersection you passed through at the start of the walk. Simply follow the signs and turn right down the small lane and then left along the road to the station, a few minutes away.

Return to Ueno by following in reverse the instructions in the "Getting There" section for this walk.

18. UME-GA-SE GORGE —————————— M

Course: Yōrō-keikoku Station → Kurogawa Marsh → Hidaka Mansion Site (Ume-ga-se Gorge) → Mt. Daifuku → Kazusa-Ōkubo Station

Reference map: Ōtaki (大多喜) and Kazusa-Nakano (上総中野) 1:25,000 Sheet Maps.

Walking time: About 3 hours 30 minutes.

Points of interest: A beautiful ravine trail, summer wildflowers and autumn colors, and the possibility of spotting monkeys.

Note: This trail can sometimes (especially in spring and summer) become quite overgrown in places, but it is not impassable.

GETTING THERE

From Platform 4 (or occasionally Platform 1) of the underground section of JR Tokyo Station, catch a local (*futsū*, 普通) Uchibō Line (内房線) train bound for Kisarazu (木更津) or Kimutsu (君津) on the Bōsō Peninsula. Get off at Goi (五井), after between 57 minutes and 1 hour 5 minutes (¥930). Currently, a suitable train leaves Tokyo at 8:44 A.M. More luxurious (and a little faster) expresses depart from Platform 1 of the Keiyō Line underground in Tokyo Station, but these have a surcharge and do not always stop at Goi. Note that Tokyo Station has similarly numbered platforms above ground, so be sure to go to the Platform 4 that is *underground*.

The alternative to this is to take any JR Sōbu Line (総武線) train from Shinjuku to Chiba (千葉), transfer to an Uchibō Line train (Platform 3 or 4) bound for Tateyama (館山) or Awakamogawa (安房鴨川), and get off at Goi.

At Goi, change to Platform 3/4, which is the Kominato Railway (小湊鉄道) to Kazusa-Nakano (上総中野). Get off at Yōrō-keikoku (養老渓谷) Station, after 1 hour 2–5 minutes. Note that not all trains go as far as Yōrō-keikoku. At the time of writing, suitable trains were leaving daily at 7:08, 9:06, and 10:10 A.M. The fare for this portion of the journey is ¥1,210, and you can buy your ticket from the conductor on this two-car diesel train.

From Yōrō-keikoku Station to Hidaka Mansion Site (1 hour 40 minutes)

As you leave by Yōrō-keikoku Station's only exit, bear right and follow the unpaved path marked "Yōrō Gorge Circular Hiking Course" (養老渓谷一周ハイキングコース), which runs parallel with the railway line. At the road encountered after a minute, bear right across the railway, then immediately right again, so that you are now going parallel to the railway but in the opposite direction to your train. Do *not* turn down the road marked "Yōrō Gorge Hiking Circular Course, Okuyōrō Bungalow Village" (養老渓谷一周ハイキングコース 奥養老バンガロー村) on your left after less than a minute. (This is an alternative walking route around popular Yōrō Gorge, but it is not recommended because it has been spoilt and is usually crowded.) Instead, go a little farther and turn left along the small bitumen (and unsignposted) road. Paddy fields lie on either side of this road, and in summer purplish *akatsumekusa* (clover) flowers line the roadside.

Within a few minutes, you will reach a steel-arch bridge painted blue that spans the Yōrō River. Bushes of *ajisai* (hydrangea) and *nemunoki* (silk tree) flowers adorn the left and right sides, respectively, of this approach to Keikoku Bridge (*Keikoku-bashi*, けいこくばし). As you cross the high structure, another bridge, known as Hōei Bridge (*Hōei-bashi*), will be visible below to the left. More interestingly, from a few meters beyond Keikoku Bridge, in the same direction you can see an old wooden water wheel. Vegetable fields and graves subsequently occupy the area to the left of the road and, a little farther on, there are houses to the right.

Although there are numerous possibilities, the easiest way to reach the Me-ga-kura Line Forest Road that leads to Ume-ga-se Gorge is to turn right down the small lane that splits off after about 7 minutes. Turn right again after a minute or so, and then right again at the main road a short distance later. A sign here indicates that this is the way to Mt. Daifuku via Me-ga-kura (大福山へ 4.0キロ 女ヶ倉聖由). On the opposite side of the road is Kurogawa Marsh (黒川沼), popular with local fishermen and noisy bullfrogs. The end of the marsh you pass has beautiful blooms of white-and-yellow *hitsujigusa* (nymphaea water lily) in summer.

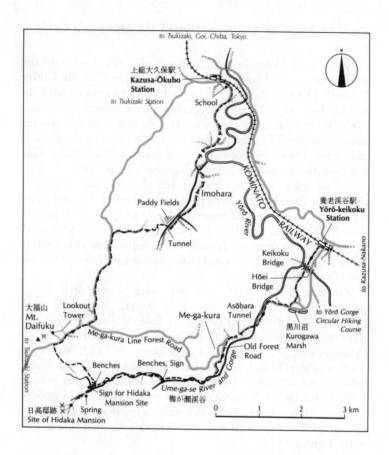

to Tsukizaki, Goi, Chiba, Tokyo

上総大久保駅
Kazusa-Ōkubo Station

to Tsukizaki Station

School

KOMINATO

Imohara

Paddy Fields

Yōrō River

Tunnel

養老渓谷駅
Yōrō-keikoku Station

RAILWAY

to Kazusa-Nakano

Keikoku Bridge

Hōei Bridge

大福山
Mt. Daifuku

Lookout Tower

Me-ga-kura

Asōbara Tunnel

黒川沼
Kurogawa Marsh

to Yōrō Gorge Circular Hiking Course

Me-ga-kura Line Forest Road

to Tsukizaki Station

Old Forest Road

River and Gorge

Benches

Benches, Sign

Ume-ga-se River and Gorge
梅が瀬渓谷

Sign for Hidaka Mansion Site

日高邸跡
Spring
Site of Hidaka Mansion

0   1   2   3 km

Hydrangea-adorned approach to Keikoku Bridge over the Yōrō River.

About 15 minutes up this forest road, which is edged with various wildflowers in summer, is Asōbara Tunnel (朝生原トンネル). Just beyond this, the old forest road veers off to the left. Follow this gravel road, past riverside construction on the left, and through a cutting. In a clearing on the right on the way, the exotic pink-fringed *nadeshiko* (dianthus wild pink) flowers in July/ August.

In less than 10 minutes the vehicle road ends, but a small walking path continues across a tiny log bridge into forest dominated by *sugi* (cedar), *hinoki* (cypress), *sakura* (cherry), *karamatsu* (Japanese larch), and *take* (bamboo). Lower down, ferns abound and yellow, brown, black, and black-and-white butterflies including *agehachō* (swallowtail) and *kuroageha* flitter from flower to flower. Among the latter are pink *kusaajisai* (hydrangea) and yellow *ōbamizohōzuki* (*Mimulus sessilifolius*). Green *amagaeru* (tree frogs) can also be found.

Soon after, you use stepping stones to cross the stream. This is the first of a series of crossings, sometimes with log bridges, as you make your way up the beautiful Ume-ga-se Gorge (*Ume-ga-se-keikoku*, 梅が瀬渓谷). Initially, the ravine is wide, and you will pass through a number of bamboo, cedar, and cypress stands. There are many birds, and in summer the forest throbs with the sound of *semi* (cicadas). At times, the path may be a little indistinct.

A little over 20 minutes from the start of the walking path, next to some rest benches, the trail turns right to follow the main valley. This point is marked by a sign indicating that this is also the way to Mt. Daifuku and Ume-ga-se Village (梅ヶ瀬渓谷へ1.1キロ 梅ヶ瀬圣由 大福山へ2.3キロ). From here, the trail can be a little overgrown, but compensations include bountiful wildflowers, particularly purple *tamaajisai* (another kind of hydrangea) and blue *akinotamurasō* (*Salvia japonica*). After skirting a small tunnel through the valley wall, you will also pass a swampy field with many tall reeds. Ignore any minor divergent tracks.

As the gorge walls draw gradually closer together (and become taller), this pretty path runs nearer the stream, and at times you will actually be walking along the drier edges of the riverbed, where there are frogs, tadpoles and *ohagurotonbo* (damsel flies). At the intersection of two ravines, after about 35 minutes, there are some benches and a choice of paths at a junction. Although your final route is to the right (unsignposted), the trail ahead up earth-and-wood steps, labeled "To Site of Hidaka Mansion" (日高邸跡へ), is an appealing short diversion that has many good places for a picnic lunch. A few minutes along this path, which follows a rocky stream bed, is an old spring with rock basins you can wash in and drink from.

About 4 minutes further on is the actual site of the former Hidaka Mansion, another rest area with a few ponds, a stone tablet, and half a dozen benches under the shade of *kaede* (maple) trees. The approach is adorned in summer with orange lilies and blue and pink Western hydrangeas. *Aoki* (laurel) trees flourish near the ponds. The several ravines that diverge at this point make excellent trails for little discoveries, although all are eventual dead ends. One of these has a beautiful river tunnel, and stands of tall bamboo are common.

From Hidaka Mansion Site to Kazusa-Ōkubo Station (1 hour 50 minutes)

Returning to the junction, turn left up the narrow valley. The path quickly climbs steeply up a spur to the right, soon passing through bamboo forest, which then changes to predominantly maple forest, making it a lovely trail in autumn. Take care along the edges of the track, as there are some precipices.

After 10–15 minutes, the trail flattens out somewhat into a smooth and leafy ridge path. I saw the first of several yellowish green snakes with black checks, possibly *aodaishō*, along here. Approximately 7 minutes later, you will arrive at a junction. Veer right, toward Mt. Daifuku (大福山へ 0.28キロ). (The trail hard to the left is marked "No Thoroughfare" [通り抜け出来ません].) You will reach the bitumen road just below the summit of Mt. Daifuku in less than 5 minutes. Turn right along the road (the other direction leads toward Tsukizaki Station [月崎駅へ 8.2キロ]). If you wish to enjoy a good view of the surrounding ridges from a nearby steel lookout tower, turn left up the signposted track toward Mt. Daifuku (*Daifuku-zan*) and Lookout Tower (*Tenbō-dai*) (大福山 展望台) less than 100 meters on. The top of the steep steps is only a few minutes away, and the tower provides a 360-degree panorama. Afterwards, return to the road.

Continuing down the bitumen road, ignore the minor dirt roads and trails leading off. In one section of the woods to the right, you can see rows of logs stacked for *shiitake* (Japanese mushroom) cultivation. Later, vegetable fields occupy both sides of the road.

In about 6 minutes, the road forks—take the quiet little bitumen alternative to the left, signposted for Tsukizaki Station (月崎駅 6.6キロ). (To the right is the Me-ga-kura Line Forest Road back to Yōrō-keikoku Station.) Giant white-and-yellow *yamayuri* (gold-banded lily), pink *shimotsuke* (spiraea), and more pink *nadeshiko* grow along this section of the walk.

About 15 minutes later, take the tiny (unsignposted) concrete road downhill to the right. (The latter part of this route can become quite overgrown, especially in spring and summer. If this might bother you, avoid this concrete road and continue on, to any of the Kominato Railway stations. Kazusa-Ōkubo is the closest station.) This ridge road becomes a gravel lane, but ceases within 10 minutes, although not before you have had the chance to see many summer wildflowers, such as white daisies, purple *u-*

tsubogusa (prunella self-heal), and yellow *kinmizuhiki* (agrimony). A narrow walking path does continue, however, straight ahead. Proceed along this.

Turn right down the (possibly overgrown) path that diverges within 20 meters, that is, leave the track that follows the ridge. Although this old trail may be difficult to follow, keep to the left and you will eventually find yourself in a hollow, and the trail soon begins to zigzag down a spur. In about 15 minutes the trail reaches a point where part of the path has been eroded. Retrace your steps a few meters and follow the small and not readily noticeable trail down the other side of the spur (to the left). Again, the track may not be very clear, but within a couple of minutes you will be in a valley, emerging beside paddy fields. Cross the stream via the nearby concrete bridge, and then turn left at the T-junction of the dirt roads a few meters on. There should be a tunnel nearby, on the road to your right.

Ignore the bitumen road leading to your right after a few minutes and walk straight on, across another bridge. Subsequently, you will pass through two tunnels, before reaching another bitumen road at a T-junction after 5 more minutes. There, bear left, in the direction signposted for Kazusa-Ōkubo Station (上総大久保駅へ 1.8キロ). This, too, is a pleasant country lane, and on one visit a troop of *nihonzaru* (macaque) descended in front of me. The route takes you over a bridge and through more tunnels, as well as past a pond, bamboo stand, various farmhouses, and fields. Toward the end of the walk, some *sakura* (cherry) trees stand near a school. There is no need to make any turns until you reach the intersection near the railway crossing, after 15–20 minutes. Swing right at this point and cross the railway, and then turn left immediately. Kazusa-Ōkubo Station is just a 100 meters or so up this road, on your left.

Return to Tokyo by following in reverse the instructions in the "Getting There" section for this walk. You should catch a train going to your right as you stand on the platform. The return fare is ¥1,140 to Goi, and ¥930 for the Goi–Tokyo leg.

19. KAMEYAMA TO KIYOSUMI —— M

Course: Kazusa-Kameyama Station → Mt. Mitsuishi → Mt. Moto-Kiyosumi turnoff → Kiyosumi Temple (by bus) → Awaamatsu Station

Reference map: Nitchi Map No. 29 (Bōsō hantō, 房総半島), Old Series No. 21.

Walking time: About 4 hours 20 minutes.

Points of interest: Broad-leaved evergreen forest, monkeys and deer, Mitsuishi Kannon and Kiyosumi temples, superb views of the Bōsō Peninsula and toward the Pacific Ocean.

GETTING THERE

From Platform 9 of Shinjuku Station, catch one of the frequent JR Sōbu Line (総武線) trains to Chiba (千葉) (1 hour 5–10 minutes). At Chiba, transfer to an Uchibō Line (内房線) local train (*futsū*, 普通) (Platform 3/4) for the 40–53 minute journey to Kisarazu (木更津). These also depart fairly often. (Although faster, Uchibō Line rapid service trains [*kaisoku*, 快速] and limited expresses [*tokkyū*, 特急]—the latter with a ¥930 surcharge—leave from Tokyo Station and stop at Kisarazu, but there is little advantage in taking one of these, since their connection with the train for the last leg is poor.)

At Kisarazu, transfer again, this time to the little Kururi Line (久留里線) diesel train (Platform 4) that consists of a single carriage. The pleasant trip through rural countryside takes 1 hour 5–10 minutes. Alight at the terminus, Kazusa-Kameyama (上総亀山). Note that, at the time of writing, only the 7:24, 9:13, and 10:06 A.M. trains were running the full distance at a suitable time.

A single ¥1,850 ticket covers the cost of all three legs.

From Kazusa-Kameyama to Mt. Mitsuishi (1 hour 15 minutes)

Leave Kazusa-Kameyama Station (where our train driver collected the tickets), turn right, and follow the small bitumen road that curves around to the right. Ignore the lane leading off to the left, and continue around to where this road merges with a larger road from the right.

A little farther on, veer left, in the direction indicated for Mt.

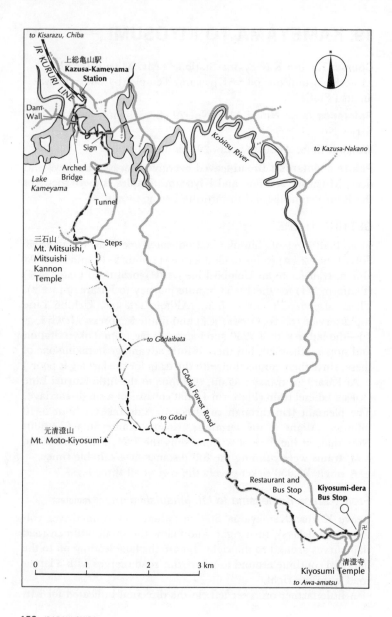

Mitsuishi (*Mitsuishi-san*, 三石山), along the road where a bridge crosses one arm of Lake Kameyama. To the right lies an attractive red arched steel bridge, also spanning this man-made body of water popular for boating and fishing and home to spot-billed ducks, swans, and other waterbirds. A short distance to the west is the wall that dams the Kobitsu River, although it is not visible from this point.

Walking on over lesser bridges, you reach a small road to the right, some 15–20 minutes from the station. Turn up this road, which is marked "Mitsuishi-san Kannon Temple" (三石山観音寺). About 15 minutes of steady climbing will bring you to a junction where a lesser, though still surfaced, road branches off to the left, through a tunnel. Take this lesser road, which eventually becomes dirt-surfaced and gradually ascends Mt. Mitsuishi. Prolific autumn wildflowers along the roadside include yellow *tanpopo* (dandelion) and *seitakaawadachisō* (tall goldenrod), black-and-yellow daisies, purple-and-yellow asters, chrysanthemums, purple Japanese mints and thistles, and red-beaded *inutade* (polygonum knotweed).

About 25 minutes from the junction, bear left up the unmarked concrete trail and steps. You should arrive at Mitsuishi Kannon Temple (named after Kannon, the Goddess of Mercy) in about 15 minutes, passing a miniature shrine during the ascent.

This old temple, dating back to the late fourteenth century and with links to the navy, is small but well sited on the summit of Mt. Mitsuishi. A short, circular concrete path that runs around this peak yields excellent views of the surrounding ranges, particularly from beside a tiny shrine on one rocky outcrop, and it is worth the walk. Other points of interest are the delicate autumn *jinjisō* (saxifraga) flowers and the stone figures on the rock faces. The temple is also popular among men who reach the fateful age of forty. Seats around the temple are plentiful, and it is suggested that you make this either a rest or lunch stop.

From Mt. Mitsuishi to Mt. Moto-Kiyosumi Turnoff (1 hour 15 minutes)

Leave the temple by the bitumen road. This leads you past several entrance gates and a bell tower. (Unusually, this bell, though of typically old design, has an automatic striker.) After approximately 5 minutes, you will meet the main road. Directly opposite, a path labeled "Kiyosumi" (清澄) leads up steep steps. Climb these and thus follow this old trail, which in places has been worn to a rocky hollow.

The path runs through plantation and evergreen trees to trace the line of ridges in the direction of Mt. Moto-Kiyosumi. Large squirrels live in the rather dark forest, and some of the trees are labeled, among them *shirakashi* (しらかし, a kind of beech) and *kusunoki* (くすのき, camphor or laurel). Occasionally there are good views of the Bōsō Peninsula's ranges of hills, which although not high are extremely rugged. The steep drop on either side of the ridges means caution is warranted.

Keep slightly right at the unmarked intersection soon encountered. In general, stay on the main path, paying attention to any signs for your final destination, Kiyosumi, and avoid the many small tracks that diverge up every minor peak and down spurs. In the absence of signs, essentially continue straight on along the ridge.

Some 45–50 minutes from the start of the path is a T-junction. To the left is Gōdaibata (郷台畑), but turn right toward Mt. Moto-Kiyosumi (*Moto-kiyosumi-yama*, 元清澄山). Again stay on the wide main track, following similar signs for Mt. Moto-Kiyosumi and generally remaining on the ridge. Ignore the large trail leading down to the right shortly after. At a point about 20 minutes from the T-junction, there is an unmarked choice of paths: one slightly uphill along the ridge, and another slightly downhill. Although it is possible to take the reasonably wide, lower of the two, which within a few minutes passes a *tsukubanegashi* (durmast) tree and its small label (つくばねがし) on the left, the main trail follows the initially smaller uphill alternative.

Within a couple of minutes, this path reaches a large signposted intersection with a mapboard. To the right, 10–15 minutes away, is the summit of Mt. Moto-Kiyosumi (元清澄山 0.9 KM). If you have sufficient time, you could walk to this peak for a look, but the description from here assumes you are following the trail essentially straight on, toward Kiyosumi Temple and its bus stop (清澄寺 バス停 7.1 KM). This is one of the Kantō Community Trails

(*Kantō fureai no michi*, 関東ふれあいの道) conveniently maintained for walkers in the Kantō District.

From Mt. Moto-Kiyosumi Turnoff to Kiyosumi Temple (1 hour 50 minutes)

Descend the steep steps with the assistance of the chains provided to proceed along this wide, well-marked path through beautiful native forest. Other trails join from the left and right, but continue straight. The many birds in this wildlife protection area include some fine singers, but probably the greatest attraction is the large number of *nihonzaru* (macaque) that inhabit the district. If they are close by the trail or in the surrounding valleys, you will probably hear their barks. Keep following signs for Kiyosumi Temple and bus stop, past turnoffs to Gōdai (郷台). Even though much of the way has handrails, care is still needed because of erosion damage. In 35–45 minutes, you should arrive at the Gōdai Forest Road where, following another sign for Kiyosumi Temple and bus stop, you veer right. The mainly gravel road allows good views of the mountains to the west and southwest (right) and provides further opportunities to encounter wild monkeys. In addition, I have spotted wild *nihonshika* (sika deer) on this little-frequented track. In autumn, blue *rindō* (gentian) flowers are common along it.

This route passes several cleared areas, and various other roads—one with an adjacent giant cedar—branch off. Ignore these roads and proceed straight on along the ridge road, noting the appropriate signs. A great variety of flora is apparent here, with white-flowered *yatsude* (an evergreen shrub, *Fatsia japonica*), *karasuzanshō* (*Fagara ailanthoides*), *fusazakura* (*Euptelea polyandra*, which has small red blossoms in spring), *kihagi* (a Lespedeza bush clover with yellow-and-purple summer-autumn flowers), *nejiki* (*Lyonia ovalifolia* var. *elliptica*, white "bells"), *teikakazura* (*Trachelospermum asiaticum*, small white flowers), and red-berried *aohada* (*Ilex macropoda*). Other attractions are the late afternoon sunset over the ranges—a glorious fusion of purple hills and a red horizon—and the distant views of the Pacific Ocean and fishing villages on the Bōsō Peninsula's east coast.

After about 1 hour, the forest road crosses over the main north-south highway running from Kame-yama to Awa-amatsu. Turn right at the T-junction a little farther on, just beyond a gate, and walk the remaining 5–10 minutes up the road to Kiyosumi Temple (*Kiyosumi-dera*). This will take you past a bus stop on the right and a restaurant with excellent views, and on the left Kiyosumidera Bus Stop and several houses.

Kiyosumi Temple is a wonderful old complex of Buddhist buildings, some thatched, one of which contains a small carving of a cow, crafted by the artist Hidari Jingorō. (He was also responsible for the famous sleeping cat of Nikkō's Tōshō Shrine, as well as other masterpieces in important centers such as Kyoto.) Ask to see "*Hidari Jingorō no ushi*" (左甚五郎の牛).

From Kiyosumi-dera Bus Stop, catch the bus to Awa-amatsu Station (安房天津駅). The journey takes approximately 20 minutes and costs ¥310. The last two buses leave at 3:37 and 6:02 P.M., so you may have considerable time to spend around the temple or in a restaurant. Alternatively, call a taxi or walk to Awa-amatsu (1 hour to 1 hour 30 minutes).

The shortest return route to Tokyo is via the Sotobō Line (外房線). These trains leave from the platform opposite that nearest the station entrance. Thus, you must cross the overhead pedestrian bridge within the station. Local trains (*futsū*, 普通) require 1 hour 50 minutes to 2 hours 20 minutes to reach Chiba, where you should transfer to the Sōbu Line (Platforms 1 and 2) for the remaining part of the journey back to Shinjuku. (Other Tokyo-bound trains leave from different platforms.) The cost of a basic ticket is ¥2,160. A faster, more comfortable limited express (*tokkyū*, 特急) also departs occasionally from Awa-amatsu Station. This gets to Tokyo Station in about two hours but has a ¥1,340 surcharge.

20. MT. WAGAKUNI ————————————— D

Course: Iwama Station → Mt. Atago → Dango Rock → Byōbu Crag → Mt. Nantai → Dōrokushin Pass → Mt. Wagakuni → Fukuhara Station

Reference map: Iwama (岩間), Kaba-san (加波山), and Haguro (羽黒) 1:25,000 Sheet Maps.

Walking time: About 5 hours 25 minutes.

Points of interest: Excellent views across Ibaraki Prefecture of the Kantō Plain and Lake Kasumi toward the Pacific Ocean, beautiful native forest and numerous wildflowers in summer, Atago Shrine.

GETTING THERE

From JR Ueno Station, take any local (*futsū*, 普通) Jōban Line (常磐線) train bound for Mito (水戸), Katsuta (勝田), Takahagi (高萩), or Taira (平). Such trains leave from Platform 10, 16, 17, or 18, depending on the time. As the full complement of cars of some trains does not complete the journey, you should get in one of the front carriages. Get off at Iwama (岩間). The trip lasts 1 hour 28–51 minutes, and the fare from Ueno is ¥1,590.

From Iwama Station to Mt. Atago (55 minutes)

Note that this first section of the walk along a bitumen road to Mt. Atago could be eliminated by taking a taxi from Iwama Station to Atago Shrine or the beginning of the path a little farther on. The cost for a group of four people would be about ¥250 per person.

To walk from Iwama Station, take the road straight ahead from its only exit (that is, the road extending perpendicularly away from the station). Pass through the traffic lights at the junction after a minute or two, but bear left at the junction a similar period later. A large overhead Lions International sign indicates that this is the way to Atago Shrine (愛宕山参道入口).

From here, just proceed straight through any intersections. You will walk under a sign for Atago Shrine Entrance (愛宕神社入口) (which is actually still quite some distance off) and between a large stand of bamboo and fields. The road begins to climb and

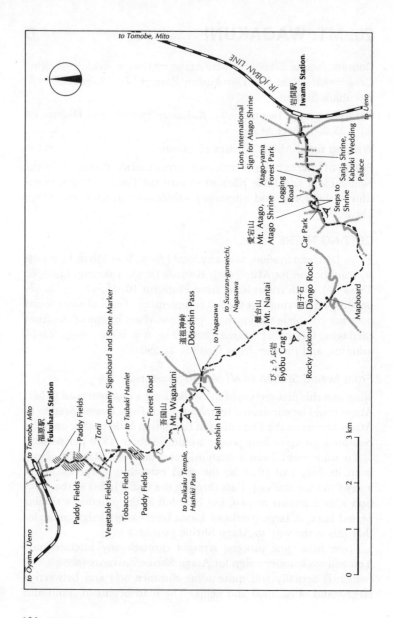

to Tomobe, Mito

JR JŌBAN LINE

岩間駅 Iwama Station.

to Ueno

Lions International
Sign for Atago Shrine

Sanja Shrine,
Kabuki Wedding
Palace

Atago-yama
Forest Park

Logging
Road

愛宕山
Mt. Atago,
Atago Shrine

Steps to
Shrine

Car Park

Mapboard

to Suzuran-gunseichi;
Nagasawa

筑波山
Mt. Nantai

団子石
Dango Rock

道祖神峠
Dōsoshin Pass

to Nagasawa

びょうぶ岩
Byōbu Crag

Rocky Lookout

Company Signboard and Stone Marker

to Tsubaki Hamlet

Forest Road

吾国山
Mt. Wagakuni

Senshin Hall

to Daikaku Temple,
Hashiki Pass

福原駅 Fukuhara Station

Paddy Fields

Paddy Fields

Torii

Vegetable Fields

Tobacco Field

Paddy Fields

to Tomobe, Mito

to Oyama, Ueno

0   1   2   3 km

A walker's prayer
at Atago Shrine.

Mt. Atago becomes visible ahead. Later you will go by the small Sanja Shrine (三社神社) and a *torii* (shrine gateway), and the large white building called "Kabuki Wedding Palace," all on the right.

A little higher are *hinoki* (cypress) plantations, and a number of summer wildflowers are ubiquitous, particularly delicate pink *murasakikatabami* (oxalis). This route also skirts the entrance to Atago-yama Forest Park (愛宕山森林公園) (where there is a map-board, another *torii*, and a stone lantern), several restaurants, and on the right side a logging road (間伐作業道 愛宕大石沢線延長). Daisies, ferns, and purplish *ajisai* (hydrangea) dot the edge of the road.

The stone stairway and *torii* leading up to the summit of Mt. Atago (*Atago-yama*, 愛宕山) are encountered on your right after about 40 minutes. Take these steep and numerous steps up to Atago Shrine, about 7 minutes away. There are good views from the summit, and the structures to the rear are interesting, including one with attractive carvings.

From Mt. Atago to Byōbu Crag (1 hour 45 minutes)

Resume the walk by taking either the Western Shrine Path (西参道) to the left (as you face the main shrine building), or the steps down to the right and then the concrete road to a bitumen road that bends around to the left. This latter route has red summer lilies on the left-hand embankment and native forest on the right. Either way, in 5–10 minutes you will arrive at a car park, around which orange lilies bloom in summer.

Follow the small bitumen road out of the other end of the car park. Small *matsu* (pine) and vines dominate this section, but you may see in summer short strings of pink-and-yellow *kihagi* (Japanese bush clover) and pink *komatsunagi* (indigo) shrub blossoms. Several minor roads lead off, but do not leave the main road until you reach the dirt forest road (unmarked at the time of writing) to the right after about 11 minutes. This turnoff is recognizable by the reforestation underway and the wide trail that rises via log-and-earth steps from the left side of this diverging forest road (just a few meters from the bitumen road).

Climb the steps. The first of many low-growing white-and-gold *terihanoibara* (wild rose) flowers can be seen in summer along this steep cleared slope. The track quickly moves into attractive native forest, and is bordered by *sasa* (dwarf bamboo). Within 10 minutes, the trail rejoins the forest road but leads off again less than a minute later. Follow this track to the right, which is signposted for Norikoshi Pass and Susuki Field (乗越峠 すすき ヶ原 25 分). The wide path passes through bamboo forest and has a wealth of summer wildflowers, including white stalks of *okatoranoo* (loosestrife), red-hot pokers, purple and pink burrs of *utsubogusa* (prunella self-heal), purple *nawashiroichigo* (a raspberry with delicious, blood-red fruit), the strangely shaped yellow-green *takatōdai* (euphorbia), and white *chidakesashi* (astilbe) "feather-dusters." Many of these can be seen along most of the rest of this trail. Another common but very beautiful summer flower is the *gibōshi* (hosta or plantain lily), whose multiple purple blooms protrude in a near-horizontal fashion. *Yamazakura* (wild cherry tree) are plentiful, too, and there is the occasional *nemunoki* (silk tree).

This path often attacks the numerous rugged slopes head-on,

resulting in a tough walk but one with superb views, particularly of Mt. Atago and parts of the Kantō Plain, and you may find the top of such a slope an excellent lunch site. Alternatively, you could wait until you get to Byōbu Crag.

After 40–45 minutes, the path meets a small bitumen road, near a picnic table with chairs cut from stone. Veer left along the road, past a mapboard and another table and chairs, for about 100 meters and then follow the continuation of the dirt track by veering off to the right. In a few minutes, you will reach Dango Rock (*Dango-ishi*, 団子石) on the right, but keep going. This ridge trail has steep up and down inclines (your progress is sometimes assisted by ropes), and the native forest has in places been supplanted by *sugi* (cedar) or *hinoki* (cypress) plantations. *Kōzo* (paper mulberry, with edible yellow fruit in summer), *sanshō* (Japanese pepper), and *mizuki* (dogwood) are also found along this trail. After 25–30 minutes, on your left you will pass a rocky lookout partly covered in summer by little white jasmine flowers, which has excellent views of the plain, before reaching the turnoff to Byōbu Crag (びょうぶ岩) approximately 5 minutes later.

The top of Byōbu Crag can be reached by following the left-hand path for less than a minute, but in any case the narrow rocky pass just below the top is a truly beautiful site that justifies a rest.

From Byōbu Crag to Mt. Wagakuni (1 hour 20 minutes)

To continue the walk, return to the intersection and take the alternative trail, signposted for Suzuran-gunseichi (literally, "place of many lilies-of-the-valley"), Mt. Wagakuni, and Nagasawa (すずらん群生地 吾国山 長沢 [3 km]). Some 10–15 minutes later, you will arrive at the 553-meter-high summit of Mt. Nantai (*Nantai-san*, 難台山), where there is a plaque showing the surrounding topography.

Continue straight on, down the steep slope on the other side of the summit. Proceed straight through the junction after 15–20 minutes, toward "Mt. Wagakuni (Senshin Hall) approximately 1.5 km" (吾国山 [洗心館] 約1.5 km). (The other path—which runs to the right—leads to Suzuran-gunseichi and Nagasawa.) There are more timber plantations and summer wildflowers, including pink *shimotsuke* (*Spiraea japonica*). Veer left onto the wide dirt track, that is, away from Nagasawa (長沢), 15–20 minutes later.

When you reach the bitumen road, just beyond a chain vehicle barrier, after a further 5 minutes, cross directly over in the direction labeled "Mt. Wagakuni" (吾国山 1.4 km 30分). This place is known as Dōsoshin Pass (*Dōsoshin-tōge*, 道祖神峠). Take the bitumen road opposite, which goes uphill. Within a few meters, a dirt pathway leads off to the left. Follow this upward, in the direction of Mt. Wagakuni and Senshin Hall, and through a thatched entrance gate. When you reach the hall after about 10 minutes, walk across the circular drive and past it, and then return to the nearby bitumen road by taking the gate on the right. The track continues close by on your left.

Follow the trail uphill, crossing directly over the road after a few minutes, toward Mt. Wagakuni Summit and Fukuhara Station (吾国山頂 福原駅). The trail remains steeply uphill all the way to the summit, about 15 minutes away, but there are many wildflowers, including those already mentioned and bright purple *azami* (thistle), more cypress plantations, and numerous birds. Among the latter are *onaga* (azure-winged magpie) and *sanshōkui* (ashy minivet).

A small shrine of stone and timber is perched on the 518-meter summit of Mt. Wagakuni (*Wagakuni-yama*, 吾国山), which is surrounded by a stone wall and entered via a few steps on your left. Various flowering shrubs, among them white wild *ajisai* (hydrangea), flank the site, and the panoramas from here are outstanding. To your left, the series of peaks you have traversed on your way here is clearly visible, and on a fine day ahead you can see Lake Kasumi (*Kasumi-ga-ura*), the long body of water extending across the Kantō Plain to the Pacific Ocean. To your right is impressive Mt. Tsukuba (*Tsukuba-san*). I was reluctant to leave this quiet and lovely spot.

From Mt. Wagakuni to Fukuhara Station (1 hour 25 minutes)

Continue past the summit, in the direction of Fukuhara (福原), down the other side. When the path forks soon after, bear right toward Fukuhara Station (*Fukuhara-eki*, 福原駅). (The other trail goes to Daikaku Temple and Hashiki Pass [大覚寺 板敷峠].) Ignore the numerous minor tracks that diverge. This forest is in places very old and boasts some magnificently tall maple, cedar, and beech trees. Numerous vines and *aoki* (laurel), some *inushide* (*Carpinus tschonoskii*), *konara* (oak), and *kasumizakura* (another kind of cherry), as well as plantation trees, grow here.

About 30 minutes from the summit, you will meet a gravel forest road. Turn right down the road and then left down the narrow and unmarked trail a few meters on. This track, which widens a little, runs through a hollow with many wildflowers. After about 8 minutes, veer left toward Fukuhara Station—note that the sign may be obscured by undergrowth. (The trail to the right leads to Tsubaki Hamlet [椿部落].)

The forest quickly becomes dark and dense, but a few minutes later you emerge and cross a small stream. Follow the trail across the paddy fields and up the slope on the far side, past a *biwa* (loquat) tree, to a bitumen road a couple of minutes away. Veer right onto the road, which on my visit had tobacco plants on the left, and subsequently bear left at the second (unpaved) vehicle track after a few more minutes. This rather inconspicuous lane is not signposted, but 30 meters or so before there is a large company signboard (facing the same direction as you are going) marked "日研機械製作所," as well as a small stone marker labeled "九丁目" below the sign. Both are on the right side of the road and may be a little overgrown. A small triangular field is next to the turnoff. (Note that there are various possible ways to Fukuhara Station. You could continue straight down the bitumen road [which leads you past fallow fields of summer red *inutade* (polygonum knotweed), a small temple, and numerous old farmhouses with thatched roofs, mud walls, and impressive entrances], and ask for directions when confronted with choices. The route described here was chosen because it maximizes your time off roads.)

This wide hollow skirts a chicken farm and then runs between fields of pumpkin, corn, beans, eggplant, and watermelon. In summer, pinkish-white *hirugao* (convolvulus) flowers spread over the edges. When you reach the *torii* and small paved road after about 6 minutes, cross straight over and proceed downhill, in the direction of Fukuhara Station. Some 3 minutes later, cross another road and continue down the concrete lane opposite. At the T-intersection after a minute or so, turn right along the road and then left at the T-junction when you are again forced to make a decision a few minutes later.

From here, simply follow this little road through a mix of paddy fields and houses for about 6 minutes to yet another T-intersection and turn left, as is signposted for Fukuhara Station. This road winds its way through the town and toward the railway line. When you reach the latter after approximately 10 minutes, follow the road around to the left (parallel with the line) to a crossing, get to the other side of the tracks, and then follow the main road back in the opposite direction (that is, to your right). In a little over 5 minutes, the small station will be visible a short distance away down a street to your right.

To return to Tokyo, you have two options, both of which involve using the Mito Line (水戸線) from Fukuhara Station to reach a Tokyo-bound line. The times required for each option are similar. The first is to take any train from the first platform as you enter the station (this is the direction of Mito [水戸] and Katsuta [勝田]) to Tomobe (友部) Station (a 15–19-minute ride), where some trains terminate. At Tomobe, transfer to Platform 1 to catch a train on the Jōban Line (the same line that you used to reach Iwama Station earlier in the day) back to Ueno Station. This will take about 5 minutes longer than the morning ride. If the train terminates at Tsuchiura (土浦), simply transfer to the next Ueno-bound train.

The second option involves catching a train from the farthest platform of Fukuhara Station to Oyama (小山), also a terminus of the Mito Line. This will take 41–48 minutes. At Oyama, transfer to any Ueno-bound (or Ikebukuro-bound, if this suits you) train on the Tōhoku Main Line (東北本線). The travel time is 1 hour 5–25 minutes.

Regardless of your return route to Ueno, the fare is ¥1,850.

MIURA PENINSULA

21. KENCHŌ TEMPLE ———————— E

Course: Kita-Kamakura Station → Kenchō Temple → Hansōbō Temple → Miharashi-dai → Ten-en (Rokkoku Pass) → Shōdo Bus Stop (by bus) → Kanazawa-Hakkei Station

Reference map: Nitchi Map No. 28 (Miura hantō, 三浦半島), Old Series No. 12.

Walking time: About 2 hours 15 minutes.

Points of interest: Kenchō Temple, Hansōbō Temple, and other Buddhist temples and Shintō shrines in the ancient capital of Kamakura, good sea views from a pleasant ridge path.

GETTING THERE

From Platform 14 of Shinagawa Station, take any JR Yokosuka Line (横須賀線) train bound for Zushi (逗子), Yokosuka (横須賀), or Kurihama (久里浜). Such trains leave about every 15 minutes. Get off at Kita-Kamakura (北鎌倉) Station, after about 45 minutes. The fare is ¥680.

From Kita-Kamakura Station to Kenchō Temple (15 minutes)

Leave Kita-Kamakura Station by walking (in the direction of the train) out the exit on the side you alighted, that is, do not cross the tracks. Walk straight on down the lane parallel to the railway, and you will soon pass on the left the entrance to Engaku Temple (*Engaku-ji*, 円覚寺), which has a famous teahouse, Butsunichi-an, that once was a lord's villa. (Engaku-ji was originally constructed in 1282, the year after the attempted invasion of Japan by the Mongols.) However, continue the few minutes down the lane to a junction. As indicated on the English-language signs, the road to the left leads up to Meigetsu Temple (*Meigetsu-in*, 明月院), known for its clusters of *ajisai* (hydrangea) blooms in June, but proceed straight on, in the direction of Kenchō Temple (*Kenchō-ji*, 建長寺),

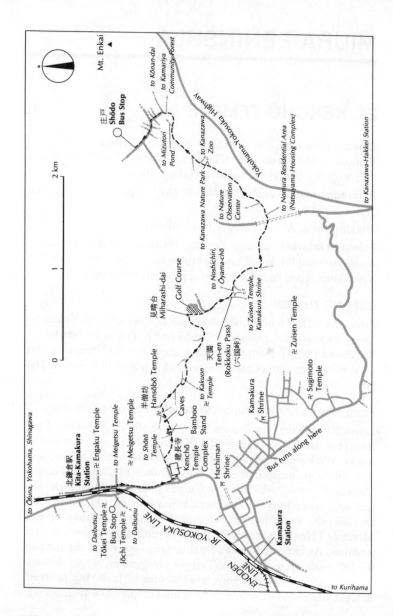

Inside Kenchō Temple.

the short distance to the intersection of the main road and the railway line.

Note, if you wish as a shorter alternative to visit the Great Buddha (*Daibutsu*, 大仏), that survivor of a tidal wave and earthquakes, you could bear right here (or even return here after visiting Kenchō Temple) and cross the railway line, then soon after turn left down the lane next to a bus stop, toward Jōchi Temple (*Jōchi-ji*, 浄智寺). That interesting walk takes a little over 1 hour, and you could stroll on to Hase (長谷) Station on the Enoden Line (江ノ島電鉄), which joins the Yokosuka Line at Kamakura (鎌倉) Station as well as the Odakyū Line (小田急線) at Fujisawa (藤沢) Station. This walk description, however, assumes that you veer left at the main road–railway intersection and follow the main road on to Kenchō Temple.

Less than 10 minutes away, next to Kamakura College, is the large entrance gate to Kenchō Temple, considered by many to be the greatest and most attractive of Kamakura's temples. This was the leading one of the five great Zen temples of Kamakura, the capital of Japan nearly eight centuries ago, and is the oldest Zen training monastery in Japan. Founded by a Chinese Zen master of the Sung Dynasty, Lan-ch'i Tao-lung (Lanqi Daolong), it was constructed by order of Emperor Gofukakusa during the regency of Hōjō Tokiyori in the thirteenth century. Although most of the original seven main buildings and forty-nine sub-temples were destroyed by fire, ten sub-temples still remain.

Pass through the gate and proceed to the *Sōmon* (General Gate), where there is an admission charge of ¥200 (¥100 for children) that includes an English-language pamphlet. Inside is the *Sanmon* (Main Gate), an impressive wooden structure with a copper roof built in 1754. The vivid white, blue, and purple summer hydrangea blooms are eye-catching, to the right especially. Also to the right hangs a temple bell cast in 1255 and designated a National Treasure. The ancient juniper trees beyond the Main Gate were planted more than seven hundred years ago from seeds brought from China. Next in line are the old *Butsuden* (Buddha Hall) and the *Hattō* (Dharma Hall), where major ceremonies are performed. Beyond the *Karamon* (Chinese Gate) is the *Hōjō* (Main Hall), which, like the *Sōmon*, was brought here from Kyoto. It is also known as the *Ryūden* (Dragon King Hall). At the rear is a Zen garden in the shape of the Chinese character for "mind."

From Kenchō Temple to Miharashi-dai (55 minutes)

The trail continues along the lane to the left of the Dharma Hall and Main Hall, in the direction of the temple offices and Hansōbō Temple (寺務所 朱印所 半僧坊). This lane runs beside an old stone wall. There are various interesting paths and temples in the vicinity. After 50 meters or so, near an old warehouse, turn right toward Hansōbō Temple and Kaishun Temple (半僧坊 回春院). (Straight ahead is Shōtō Temple [正統院].) This way takes you along an attractive stone path between houses and forest with several kinds of hydrangea.

Shortly after, continue straight ahead in the direction of Hansōbō Temple (半僧坊). The trail passes a large bamboo stand and some *yagura* (Buddhist memorial caves peculiar to Kamakura), and through *torii* (shrine gateways), as well as forest, stone lanterns, and giant tablets erected in honor of various donors. Up the stone steps, some 10–15 minutes from Kenchō Temple, is Hansōbō Temple, relocated from Shizuoka Prefecture and guarded by bronze *tengu* (long-nosed goblins). From this bluff, the views of Sagami Bay to the southwest are good.

The trail resumes up the steps between the stone *torii* to the right of Hansōbō Temple. About 5 minutes later, you will reach the top of the ridge, where there is an intersection. Proceed straight on, in the direction of "Zuisen and Kakuon temples (Ten-en Hiking Course)" (瑞泉寺 覚園寺方面 [天園ハイキングコース]), along the ridge path through bamboo. Houses should be visible below to the left, and more good views of the bay are on offer to the right. Evidence of small-scale quarrying and a lookout lie on the immediate left of the path. Keep straight, along the ridge, toward Ten-en (天園) at the junction with a track from the right after less than 10 minutes. Some of the (unmarked) minor trails that diverge lead quickly to good vantage points.

Many birds make their home in this belt of mostly native forest, which includes a wealth of evergreens, such as laurels, and you may well see kites circling as they look for prey. As the center of Japan's feudal military government and culture from 1192 to 1333, the Kamakura area is a mecca for temple buffs and contains numerous historical and religious sites of various sizes. One such site is the little burial cave and statue on the left encountered during this section of the trail. Approximately 5 minutes past the junction (follow the main path by descending the few steps from the rock ledge and, shortly after, going along the primary track), turn right in the (possibly currently unsignposted) direction of Ten-en. A couple of minutes later, continue straight through the crossroads in the direction of Zuisen Temple via Ten-en (瑞泉寺 [天園を圣て]). (To the right is Kakuon Temple [*Kakuon-ji*, 覚園寺], 10–15 minutes away. As another alternative, you could walk from there down to Kamakura Station, another 30–40 minutes.)

The trail continues along the ridge, occasionally with a brief steep climb or descent and in places as a hollow, revealing the path's great age. Ferns and, in summer, the occasional long white strand of *okatoranoo* (chlethra loosestrife), mauvish white bells of *hotarubukuro* (bellflower), and, more prolifically, vines of pink *hirugao* (convolvulus) flowers flourish between coniferous trees to the side. After 20–25 minutes, you will arrive at Miharashi-dai (見晴台), a viewing point with chairs adjacent to a golf course and clubhouse and overlooking the bay.

From Miharashi-dai to Shōdo (1 hour 5 minutes)

Descend the other side of this hill, pass through the clearing with more chairs, and then walk up the gravel road in the direction of Kamakura Shrine and Zuisen Temple (鎌倉宮 瑞泉寺).

The continuation of the trail leads you to a fork just meters before the high ground at Ten-en (Rokkoku Pass) (天園 [六国峠山頂]) after 7 minutes or so. There are tables and chairs here, and refreshments are sold.

You can go left at the fork, around the back of the tables and chairs, or continue on 50 meters to the next fork and then go left. (Incidentally, the paths straight on and—a few meters on after you have turned left—to the right both lead in the direction of Zuisen Temple and Kamakura Shrine [瑞泉寺 鎌倉宮方面]. Zuisen Temple is famous for its Zen gardens and seasonal flowers—narcissus in January, plum blossoms in February, peonies in May, Chinese bellflowers in June–August, *hagi* [bushclover] in September, and maple leaves in November—while Kamakura Shrine boasts torchlight Nō plays, performed in open-air surroundings on the evenings of September 21 and 22. If you wish to visit these and other nearby temples and shrines, you could continue on down to the main road and walk or catch a bus to Kamakura Station.)

These two alternatives meet within a minute or two, and about 20 meters downhill you should go straight through the intersection with a path to the left, toward Asahina and Kanazawa Community Forest (朝比奈 金沢市民の森). (The track to the left heads toward Noshichiri and Ōyama-chō [野七里 大山町].) Ignore the additional path soon after to Kamakura Shrine and Zuisen Temple (鎌倉宮 瑞泉寺方面) to the right, and keep left (downhill) on the main path at the unsignposted fork 8–10 minutes later.

The view on the left is dominated by glimpses of the huge Yokohama Cemetery and, somewhat incongruously, a large white garbage incineration plant, but the path remains on the ridge, passing through patches of quiet and attractive native forest with birds, skinks, and large black butterflies. You will pass through several stone cuttings, and actually cross over the vehicle tunnel used by the bus to Kanazawa-Hakkei Station, which you will catch at the end of the walk.

At the junction reached after 10–15 minutes, continue on in the direction of Yokohama Nature Observation Forest (横浜自然観察の森). (A trail to Nomura Residential Area [Natsuyama Housing Complex] [野村住宅 (夏山団地)] departs to the right.) A few minutes later, a track to a nature observation center (自然観察センター) veers off to the left, but proceed straight on toward Kōnan-dai and Mt. Enkai (港南台 円海山方面).

The path becomes wider and more open and passes several boards that show the forest's features, which include *mizuki* (dogwood), *konara* (a kind of beech), *kashi* (evergreen oak), and *kunugi* (another kind of oak) trees, *nogiku* (aster) and *tanpopo* (dandelion) wildflowers, and *uguisu* (bush warbler) birds.

There are various tracks signposted to the right (to Kanazawa Nature Park [金沢自然公園], Kanazawa Zoo [金沢動物園], and Kamariya Community Forest [釜利谷市民の森へ]) and to the left (to the Nature Observation Center and Mizutori Pond [水鳥の池])—all of which might be interesting diversions—but continue along the main trail past these until you reach the turnoff on the left to Shōdo Residential Area and Bus Stop (庄戸住宅 バス停), after about 15 minutes. Shōdo Bus Stop is just 15 more minutes away. (The main path continues straight ahead in the direction of Kōnan-dai [港南台方面] and, eventually [less than an hour away], Mt. Enkai [*Enkai-zan*, 円海山], from about 15 minutes beyond which it is also possible to catch a bus. In some places, the main path is also indicated as being toward Hitori-sawa and Segami Community Forest [氷取沢 瀬上市民の森へ].)

Descend the concrete steps, which in summer are flanked by hydrangea blooms, and then walk straight down the small bitumen road until you reach the main road at a T-junction. There cross the road at the pedestrian crossing, and turn left and follow this road downhill past a playground on your right. You will pass straight through a major junction and, 100 meters later, reach the bus stop.

Kanagawa Chūō Kōtsū buses leave reasonably regularly (except between about 2:00 and 4:00 P.M.) and until quite late for Kanazawa-Hakkei (金沢八景), and the terminus is close to Kanazawa-Hakkei Station (金沢八景駅), which is on the Keikyū Line (京急線), also known as the Keihin Kyūkō Line. Get on at the front of the bus, and pay as you board. The 25-minute, ¥200 trip takes you back past the cemetery, through a tunnel, and then under the Yokohama-Yokosuka Highway. After alighting at the last stop, walk the few meters to the traffic lights and turn left. The station is less than 100 meters away, straight ahead.

From Kanazawa-Hakkei Station, take a limited express (tokkyū, 特急) or an express (kyūkō, 急行) back to Shinagawa (about 40 minutes by the faster, limited express). Alternatively, if the timing is suitable, transfer at the next station, Kanazawa-Bunko (金沢文庫), to an even faster rapid limited express (kaisoku tokkyū, 快速特急) to Shinagawa. The fare in any case is ¥500.

TANZAWA

22. Ō MOUNTAIN ───────────────── D

Course: Hadano Station (by bus) → Minoge Bus Terminus → Yabitsu Pass → Ō Mountain → Miharashi-dai → Hinata-yakushi Bus Terminus (by bus) → Isehara Station

Reference map: Nitchi Map No. 24 (Tanzawa sankei, 丹沢山塊), Old Series No. 5; or Shōbunsha Map No. 21 (Tanzawa, 丹沢), Old Series No. 19.

Walking time: About 4 hours 5 minutes.

Points of interest: Excellent views of Mt. Fuji, Izu and Miura Peninsulas, and the Kantō Plain, Hinata-yakushi Temple.

Note: This walk can be shortened (thus reducing its rating to "M") by catching a bus from Hadano Station to Yabitsu-tōge (see details below).

GETTING THERE

From Shinjuku Station, take an Odakyū Line (小田急線) express (*kyūkō*, 急行) from Platform 4 or 5 to Hadano (秦野) Station, also known as Ōhatano (大秦野) Station. As the Odakyū Line branches at Sagami-Ōno (相模大野) Station, make sure you are on a train bound for Odawara (小田原) or Hakone-Yumoto (箱根湯本) and *not* Enoshima (江ノ島). Also, some trains divide at Sagami-Ōno, with the front and rear having different destinations, so be sure to board one of the front carriages. The trip usually takes about 1 hour 10 minutes, and the fare is ¥570.

Walk straight out of the exit at Hadano Station and over the pedestrian crossing to Bus Stand No. 2. There, catch one of the fairly frequent No. 20 Kanagawa Chūō Kōtsū buses bound for Minoge (蓑毛). Get off at the terminus, after 15–20 minutes (¥220).

(*To shorten this walk by about 1 hour 5 minutes, from the same bus stand outside Hadano Station catch a bus to Yabitsu-tōge [ヤビツ峠] [45–50 minutes, ¥420]. The only suitable departures

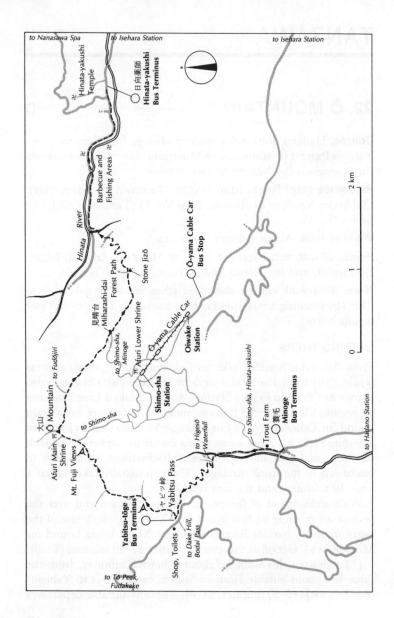

Hinata-yakushi Temple
日向薬師

日向薬師 **Hinata-yakushi Bus Terminus**

N

Barbecue and Fishing Areas

Hinata River

Hinata

Ō-yama Cable Car Bus Stop

2 km

見晴台 Miharashi-dai Forest Path

Stone Jizō

to Shimo-sha, Minoge

Ō-yama Cable Car

卍 Afuri Lower Shrine

Oiwake Station

1

Shimo-sha Station

to Fudōjiri

to Shimo-sha, Hinata-yakushi

大山 ○ **Mountain**

to Shimo-sha

Afuri Main Shrine

Mt. Fuji Views

to Higeso Waterfall

養毛 Trout Farm

Minoge Bus Terminus

to Hadano Station

ヤビツ峠 Yabitsu Pass

Yabitsu-tōge Bus Terminus

to Dake Hill, Bodai Pass

0

to To Peak, Fudakake

at the time of writing were daily at 8:55 A.M. and at 8:15 A.M. on Sundays and holidays.)

A ticket known as the "Tanzawa Ō-yama Free Pass" that permits travel on transport described for this walk is available from the Odakyū Line ticket office at Shinjuku. B-Tickets (*B-kippu*) cost ¥1,440 (¥730 for children) and allow return travel by train from Shinjuku and the use of local buses. A-Tickets (*A-kippu*) are ¥2,010 (¥1,020) and additionally include use of the Ō-yama Cable Car. The benefit derives from convenience rather than any great saving.

From Minoge to Yabitsu Pass (1 hour 5 minutes)

From Minoge Bus Terminus, cross the road and go up the small, bitumen lane to the right, immediately before the bridge. Signposts indicate that this is the direction of Shimo-sha and Hinata-yakushi (下社 日向薬師) and of a shortcut to Yabitsu Pass (ヤビツ峠近道). The lane runs beside a stream, past bamboo stands and a trout farm, to a small fork a few minutes away. Keep to the left on the concrete lane toward "Tanzawa's Yabitsu Pass" (丹沢ヤビツ峠), and ignore the smaller walking path straight ahead to Shimo-sha and Hinata-yakushi. (Note that as Hinata-yakushi Temple is actually your final destination, via Miharashi-dai, this is actually an alternative route that bypasses the summit of Ō Mountain.)

About 15 minutes later, after passing a campsite, the lane ends and a quiet walking trail commences with a narrow wooden bridge across the stream. A signpost here confirms this to be the way to Yabitsu Pass (*Yabitsu-tōge*, ヤビツ峠). Follow the dirt path on the other side of the water through plantation up the slope, ignoring the dead-end turnoff to Higesō Waterfall (髭僧の滝 [行キ止リ]) and the various minor, unmarked branches, many of which are just rough shortcuts across loops in the path. This trail lies, as does the entire route described, within the Tanzawa-Ō-yama National Park.

As you gain altitude, the view of the ocean, generally to your rear, will become wider. Initially, Sagami Bay and Ō-shima, the island to the south, are visible, but gradually the slightly more westerly Izu Peninsula will also be discernible. The forest changes to a beautiful mix of native species, including maples. Birds to watch for include *kawarahiwa* (oriental greenfinch), *shijūkara* (great tit), *aoji* (black-faced bunting), *hōjiro* (siberian meadow bunting), and *uguisu* (bush warbler).

There is more plantation and then a mix of native forest and plantation, and after approximately 45 minutes you reach a major but unsignposted fork. Although the upper path leads to Ō Mountain, you can walk the one hundred meters or so along the lower, left-hand path to the bitumen road running through Yabitsu Pass. To the right down the road are situated a shop and toilets on the left and the stop for the bus from Hadano Station on the right. A sign in this direction shows that the road heads to Tō Peak and Fudakake (塔ノ岳 札掛), and up steps to the left begins a trail to Dake Hill and Bodai Pass (岳の台ハイキングコース 菩提峠).

From Yabitsu Pass to Ō Mountain (1 hour 10 minutes)

At the pass, take the path marked "Ō Mountain" (*Ō-yama*, 大山) that leads uphill from near the bus stop. Within a minute or two, this skirts a mountain lodge. At the fork immediately thereafter, veer left up the slope, toward Ō Mountain. The trail, initially up rock-and-timber steps, wends its way to the summit of sacred Ō Mountain in a series of steep climbs up Itatsumi Ridge. These are connected by flatter stretches, and in one case a small chain-assisted descent, and along the way you pass a number of tables and benches suitable for resting or lunching.

As you ascend, the southern panorama widens to include Kanagawa and Miura Peninsula and beyond, while to the west the magnificent cone of Mt. Fuji is slowly revealed. To the left and below, a bare patch on top of a minor peak where hang gliders are launched should become visible. Mt. Fuji is hidden behind an intermediate mountain at one stage but higher up reappears even more spectacularly. Again ignore the minor branches and trail shortcuts and just follow the signs for Ō Mountain.

After about 55 minutes, the trail merges with another from the right but continue uphill. (This other track comes from Shimo-sha—a path to which you passed at the beginning of the walk. Shimo-sha is the upper terminus of the Ō-yama Cable Car. Consequently, the number of walkers will probably increase beyond this point.)

Some 5–10 minutes later, you walk through a metal *torii* (shrine gateway) and, soon after, a second *torii*. Up the stone steps is the main building of Afuri Shrine (阿夫利神社本社). (The lower part of this shrine, halfway down the mountain at Shimo-sha, is believed to have been established in 7 B.C. as an imperial shrine. Worshipers pray there for rain, when it is needed.) Up more steps are various buildings and rest points. This relatively small, 1,252-meter-high summit provides superb vistas to the east, across the heavily populated Kantō Plain to Tokyo, Yokohama, and on some days beyond, to Chiba and Bōsō Peninsula. You should even be able to pick out Tokyo's major centers such as Shinjuku, and Marunouchi, and Ikebukuro's tall Sunshine Sixty Building.

From Ō Mountain to Hinata-yakushi (1 hour 50 minutes)

An alternative but busier route for those interested in visiting the lower branch of Afuri Shrine involves returning to the junction about 10 minutes below the summit of Ō Mountain and keeping left, toward Shimo-sha (literally, "Lower Shrine"). A descent of about 1 hour, keeping left at the major intersection encountered (unless you wish to return to Minoge), will take you to the shrine and Shimo-sha Cable Car Station. From there, either ride the cable car (¥350) the two stations to the lower terminus, Oiwake, or walk for about 40 minutes past Ō-yama Temple to Oiwake Station. A bus for Isehara Station (伊勢原駅) leaves from down the road (25–30 minutes, ¥260).

However, to complete the walk described here, take the relatively quiet, steep downhill path, marked "Direction of Miharashi-dai" (見晴台方面), from Ō Mountain's summit. This is also the way to Fudōjiri (不動尻). Much of the native forest is beech, and there are intermittent views of the temples farther down the mountain.

At the junction after about 15 minutes, proceed straight on, toward Miharashi-dai (見晴台). (The trail to the left leads to Fudō-jiri and, later, Kōtakuji Spa [広沢寺温泉]. Details of this spa are provided in the Tanzawa section of *Day Walks Near Tokyo*.) The trail is rocky in places and continues to drop steeply with the occasional flat or upward section, and in 30–35 minutes you will arrive at Miharashi-dai (meaning "Lookout Point"), which offers a rest

Superb Mt. Fuji panorama on the trail from Yabitsu Pass to Ō Mountain.

shelter, tables and benches, and good views. The path to the right heads back to Shimo-sha and eventually to Minoge, but keep straight on in the direction of Hinata-yakushi (日向薬師).

Ignore the forest path to the left (ふれあいの森 管理棟) after 10–15 minutes, and then turn left toward Hinata-yakushi at the T-junction soon after. A large stone Jizō (the guardian deity of children and travelers) with a cap and red bib marks this point. The path then zigzags for 20 minutes down to a bitumen road, which you should cross over. Descend the rocky steps on the other side of the road, in the direction labeled for Hinata-yakushi. Less than 10 minutes later, the leafy trail crosses, via a narrow bridge, a small stream and then meets the main road. Bear right and follow this road, which parallels the Hinata River, down past fishing sites, restaurants, temples, paddy and vegetable fields, and houses.

Ignore any turnoffs, and in 20–25 minutes you will reach Hinata-yakushi Bus Terminus on the right. Buses leave for Isehara Station (伊勢原駅) about every 20 minutes, and the fare for the 25–30 minute journey is ¥240. If you wish to have a look at

Hinata-yakushi Temple, which dates back to the eighth century and was named after Yakushi, the Buddha of Healing, continue the short distance past the bus terminus to a signposted lane that diverges to the left. It is a 15-minute walk up to the once-remote mountain temple, which has a thatched roof and a wooden statue of Buddha. People with eye problems visit the temple in the hope of being cured.

Return to Shinjuku by Odakyū Line express from Isehara Station (¥490).

TAKAO

23. SOUTHERN TAKAO RIDGE ——— M
(or D, if lengthened)

Course: Takao-san-guchi Station (by bus) → Ōtarumi Pass → Mt. Daido → vicinity of Mt. Nakazawa → Nishiyama Pass → Misawa Pass → Takao-san-guchi Station

Reference map: Nitchi Map No. 23 (Jinba Takao, 陣馬 高尾), Old Series No. 4; or Shōbunsha Map No. 22 (Takao Jinba, 高尾 陣馬), Old Series No. 20.

Walking time: About 3 hours 20 minutes (or 5 hours 10 minutes with the lengthened start).

Points of interest: Mixed forests, autumn colors, spring and summer wildflowers, views of Lake Tsukui and Lake Shiroyama.

Note: The walking time and difficulty rating for this walk assume you take buses to the start of the trail.

GETTING THERE

From Platform 3 (or, occasionally, Platform 2) of the Keiō Line section of Shinjuku Station, catch a Keiō Line (京王線) limited express (*tokkyū*, 特急) or express (*kyūkō*, 急行) bound for Takao-san-guchi (高尾山口), and get off at the terminus. Limited expresses leave about every 20 minutes, with an express departing in between. These trains take about 47 and 53 minutes, respectively. Do not confuse Takao-san-guchi with the station before (Takao, 高尾). Be sure *not* to catch a train for the other major destination, Keiō-Hachiōji (京王八王子), unless it is one of the limited expresses that go to both places by dividing at Takahatafudō (高幡不動). In this case you should get in one of the rear carriages. A ticket to Takao-san-guchi costs ¥370.

It is also possible to take the JR Chūō Line (中央線) to Takao Station and then transfer to the Keiō Line for the last part of the ride.

As you leave the ticket gate at Takao-san-guchi Station, turn left and walk the few meters to the bus stop. There, board a Kanagawa Chūō Kōtsū bus bound for Sagami-ko-eki (相模湖駅). After 15–20 minutes, alight at *Ōtarumi-tōge* (Ōtarumi Pass, 大垂水峠) Bus Stop. The fare is ¥210.

If the infrequent bus schedule is inconvenient (the only practical departure in the past has been at about 9:45 A.M.), it is possible to take a taxi or to walk to Ōtarumi Pass by following the path outlined in the following section. While adding considerable time to the suggested walk, this trail is excellent for its wildflowers, birds, and native forest, especially in autumn when the maples provide a dazzling display of color. This alternative is described below.

Walking Alternative to the Bus to Ōtarumi Pass (1 hour 40 minutes–2 hours)

Turn right when coming out of the station and follow the small lane around to the right for a few minutes to the Mt. Takao cable car and chairlift stations. To the left of these, a trail leads across a small bridge and then up steps. Walk up this occasionally steep path, known as the Mt. Inari Course (稲荷山コース), which is part of a walk described in *Day Walks Near Tokyo*. Stay on the main path, which soon passes a small shrine and later several rest or observation points, including one offering superb views of Mt. Fuji.

Just before the final steps to the summit of Mt. Takao, 50–60 minutes from the start of the path, you will reach an intersection with paths veering to the right and left, both of which are part of Mt. Takao's Nature Study Trail No. 5. Take the left-hand track, marked "Itchō Plain and Mt. Shiro" (一丁平 城山), thus skirting the summit of Mt. Takao. On the sides of paths in this area grow various kinds of strawberry and raspberry, as well as a few mulberry trees that bear fruit in late spring and early summer. Wildflowers at this latter time include mauvish *hotarubukuro* (bellflower) and white *okatoranoo* (loosestrife).

Approximately 5 minutes later at a large, five-way intersection, veer left again, this time toward Ōtarumi Pass (*Ōtarumi-tōge*, 大垂水峠). The forest on the sides of the path to the pass gradually changes from naturally occurring *momi* (fir), *buna* (beech), and *kashi* (oak) trees to a mixture of natural growth and planted *sugi*

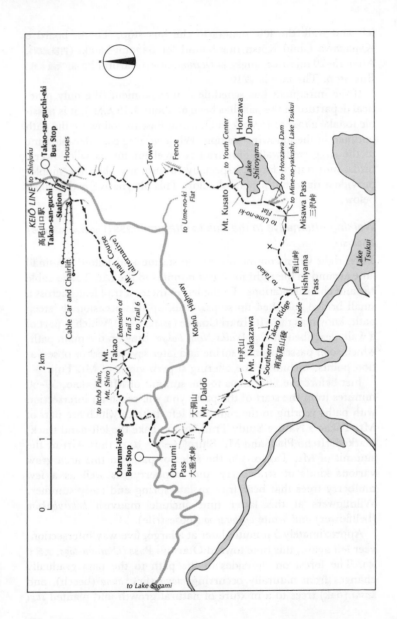

(cedar) and *hinoki* (cypress). After a further 5–7 minutes, just past another rest shelter, bear hard right downhill in the direction of Ōtarumi Pass (as signposted—but none too clearly—on a tree).

From here, simply follow similar signs. This will involve veering left after 7–10 minutes, turning right onto a forest road 15–20 minutes later, and finally veering left down a small path after another 5 minutes. White *dokudami* (the perennial *Houttuynia cordata*) and blue *tsuyukusa* (dayflower) are among the more common of the many wildflowers here, in addition to the spring blossoms of *yamazakura* (wild cherry).

The pass, through which Kōshū Highway (*Kōshū-kaidō*) runs, is reached 10–15 minutes later. Walk down the steps, cross the highway, and continue up the other side through the signposted break in the fence. Subsequent details of the walk are provided in the following sections.

From Ōtarumi Pass to Mt. Nakazawa Vicinity (1 hour)

Assuming you arrived at Ōtarumi Pass by bus, the start of the trail is reached by walking back along the highway, on the same side as you alighted, toward Takao-san-guchi Station. After about 150 meters, veer right uphill, through the break in the fence. A sign here announces that this is way to the Southern Takao Ridge (南高尾山稜) and also the direction of Ume-no-ki Flat, Mine-no-yakushi Temple, and Mt. Hatsuzawa (梅ノ木平 峰ノ薬師 初沢山). This is the beginning of a trail that, although close to popular Mt. Takao, is relatively little used.

Follow this path across a cleared, ferny slope eroded in places and then climb upward. This leads you to a minor intersection near a road, from where you take the main path up to a T-junction about 10 minutes from Ōtarumi Pass. Turn left at this junction. Signs for the S1 Course (S1コース) and Mt. Daido, Mt. Nakazawa, and Ume-no-ki Flat (大洞山 中沢山 梅ノ木平) indicate the way.

Kojukei (bamboo partridge) frequent this area of many wildflowers, such as white *jūnihitoe* (bugle), purple *nigakusa* (*Teucrium japonicum*) and *tatsunamisō* (skullcap), yellow *nigana* (ixeris), and *natsutōdai* (a euphorbia with small, spiderlike appendages), and flowering shrubs, among which are *kamatsuka* (*Pourthiaea villosa*).

Misty valley scene along the path to Ōtarumi Pass.

The *sasa*(dwarf bamboo)-bordered trail persists uphill for about 15 minutes, crossing or passing several tracks, until it meets the Southern Takao Ridge, where you should bear left, as indicated by the sign. This is also an excellent place for wildflowers: white *ajisai* (hydrangea), purple-blue *hotarukazura* (gromwell or puccoon), and the exotic, white *ikarisō* (barrenwort); edible *warabi* (bracken) also grows here.

A few minutes away is the summit of Mt. Daido (*Daido-zan*), but it is not especially interesting, so keep going. The trail soon begins to wander up and down—occasionally steeply. Veer left where it descends into forest some minutes beyond Mt. Daido and go straight through the signposted intersection immediately after.

Signs similar to the earlier ones make staying on the path relatively easy. About 20 minutes later is a minor summit that wild pink *tsutsuji* (azalea) adorns in April and May. The cleared area just before this peak makes a good lunch site, with enjoyable views of the Takao range to the north.

From the minor summit, descend to the right, signposted as usual. The trail heading up sharply to the left at the intersection about 7 minutes later leads to the summit of Mt. Nakazawa, but continue on the main path.

From Mt. Nakazawa Vicinity to Takao-san-guchi Station (2 hours 20 minutes)

Other signs on the main path, which passes through forest, indicate that this is also the direction of Nishiyama Pass (西山峠) and Misawa Pass (三沢峠方面). Wild strawberries and raspberries including *fuyuichigo* and maroon-flowered *nawashiroichigo* (the fruit of both are edible) abound, and there are good, elevated views of Lake Tsukui (津久井湖) and the Tanzawa range to the southwest.

The intersection at Nishiyama Pass (*Nishiyama-tōge*), 30–35 minutes later, has paths to Takao (高尾) to the left and to Nade (名手) to the right, but go straight. About 5 minutes later the path splits, with the left-hand track, marked "Ridge Course" (山稜コース), "Precipitous Slope" (急な坂道あり), and "Strong Walkers' Course (S1)" (健脚コース [S1]), ascending. Avoid this slippery way by taking the lower trail, with a near illegible signpost, slightly to the right.

The track to the left (境界線 行どまり) 6 minutes or so later represents a boundary line and is a dead end. The trail splits again a couple of times (the lower alternatives are easiest), before reaching a major intersection after less than 10 minutes. This is Misawa Pass (*Misawa-tōge*). The tables and benches here make it a suitable spot for a rest, and there is a mapboard.

To the left is a "Kantō Community Path" (関東ふれあいの道) to Ume-no-ki Flat (*Ume-no-ki-daira*, 梅の木平), while the way almost straight ahead is an extension of this community path to Mine-no-yakushi (about a 20-minute walk) and Lake Tsukui (峰ノ薬師へのみち 津久井湖), but follow the path in between these (that is, slightly to the left) toward Lake Shiroyama (城山湖). A nearby second sign confirms that this is also the way to Takao-san-guchi Station (高尾山口駅).

Within 5 minutes, this section of the trail, with deciduous forest that is very pretty in autumn, passes by a loop in a road down to Honzawa Dam (本沢ダム) across the most easterly reach of Lake Shiroyama. Subsequently, excellent views of this lake can be had to the right. This section is also precipitous, and there are ropes to assist hikers on some of the steeper sections. Autumn wildflowers beside this track are white *senninsō* (traveler's-joy) and *sarashinashōma* (cohosh), and purple *yamatorikabuto* (aconite or Japanese monkhood).

On top of the low peak of Kusato-yama (草戸山), 15–20 minutes further on, is a choice of paths. Ignore the path slightly to the right to a youth center (青少年センター至), and veer left down the slope to stay on the main path. Some 6–8 minutes later, at a junction with a track to the left, turn left toward Ume-no-ki Flat and Takao-san-guchi. From here, simply follow the signs for Takao-san-guchi Station or similar, turning left at one junction near a fence after about 8 minutes, and then left again after another 8 minutes, past an old steel tower.

The walk along this ridge provides good views of Mt. Takao that are particularly pretty when the golden hues of autumn leaves contrast with the deep greens of evergreen forest. Some 20–25 minutes later at a major intersection, bear left toward Takao-san-guchi Station, as signposted. This path descends rapidly to houses in Takao Town. Turn right after approximately 7 minutes at the T-junction between houses, and then left soon after. At the highway a few meters away, turn right and walk to the traffic lights, where you should cross over. The station is across the river on your left.

Return to Tokyo via the Keiō Line to Shinjuku, following in reverse the instructions provided in the "Getting There" section for this walk.

OKUTAMA

24. MITSUKAMA FALLS ———————— M

Course: Okutama Station or Shiromaru Station → Mitsukama Falls → Ōnara Pass → Hatonosu Station

Reference map: Nitchi Map No. 21 (Okutama, 奥多摩), Old Series No. 2; or Shōbunsha Map No. 24 (Okutama), Old Series No. 24.

Walking time: About 3 hours 35 minutes.

Points of interest: The spectacular three tiers of Mitsukama Falls, surrounding native forest, good valley views, spring and summer wildflowers, including the exotic *katakuri*.

GETTING THERE

Ideally, go by one of the occasional direct special rapid service trains (*chokutsū tokubetsu kaisoku*, 直通特別快速) that leave on Sundays and public holidays in the warmer months from Platform 5 of JR Shinjuku Station for Okutama (奥多摩). Get off at the terminus, a journey of 1 hour 26–34 minutes. Only the first half of the train completes the entire journey to Okutama, so be sure to board one of the front carriages.

Another possibility is to catch, from Platform 8 of the same station, one of the frequent Chūō Line (中央線) rapid service (*kaisoku*, 快速) or special rapid service (*tokubetsu kaisoku*, 特別快速) trains bound for Tachikawa (立川) Station (38 and 27 minutes, respectively) or farther. At Tachikawa, change to Platform 2/3, which serves the JR Ōme Line (青梅線) to Okutama, the terminus (1 hour 7–18 minutes' traveling time). Note that not all trains go the full distance to Okutama, so board a suitable one. You can also alight at Shiromaru (白丸), the station before Okutama.

It is most economical to buy a cheap return (Tokyo Area–Okutama–Akikawa–Tokyo Area) ticket, known as an *Okutama-Akikawa jiyūkippu*, literally "freedom ticket," which can in fact be used for destinations anywhere along the JR Ōme and Itsukaichi

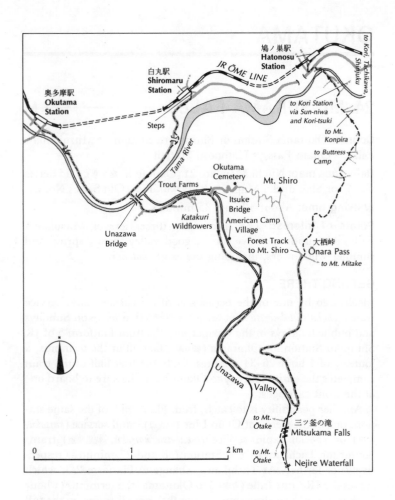

奥多摩駅
**Okutama
Station**

白丸駅
**Shiromaru
Station**

Steps

JR ŌME LINE

鳩ノ巣駅
**Hatonosu
Station**

to Kori, Tachikawa, Shinjuku

to Kori Station
via Sun-niwa
and Kori-tsuki

to Mt.
Konpira

to Buttress
Camp

Tama River

Okutama
Cemetery

Mt. Shiro

Trout Farms

Itsuke
Bridge

Katakuri
Wildflowers

American Camp
Village

Forest Track
to Mt. Shiro

Unazawa
Bridge

大栖峠
Ōnara Pass

to Mt. Mitake

Unazawa

Valley

*to Mt.
Ōtake*

三ツ釜の滝
Mitsukama Falls

*to Mt.
Ōtake*

Nejire Waterfall

N

0   1   2 km

lines for two days. This ticket costs ¥1,440 (for journeys beginning at Shinjuku, Shibuya, and Ikebukuro) or ¥1,740 (from Tokyo and Ueno) and is available at most JR stations. If you wish to buy just a one-way ticket, the fare from Shinjuku to Okutama or Shiromaru is ¥1,030.

From Okutama or Shiromaru Station to Mitsukama Falls (1 hour 20 minutes)

Leave Okutama Station by the only exit (retain your *jiyūkippu* if you have one), walk to the main road, and turn left. Follow the main road through the intersection after a minute or two, back toward Shiromaru, thus staying high on the same side of the river. Avoid the vehicle tunnel by taking the road around it to the right. After 15–20 minutes you will reach Unazawa Bridge (うなざわばし), a concrete arch structure, on your right.

If you alighted at Shiromaru Station, take the little concrete path and steps at the rear of the platform (near the railway crossing) steeply down to a bitumen road and follow this around to the right to the main road. When you reach the main road after a minute or two, cross to the other side and walk to your right along it, high above the beautiful Tama River. The tunnel you will encounter can be avoided by taking the small dirt road that veers off to the left just before and rejoins a little farther on. Numerous spring wildflowers grow along the river bank, including yellow and mauve *kikeman* (corydalis) and pink *tsubaki* (camellia). You will pass some buildings and reach Unazawa Bridge on your left after 15–20 minutes.

Turn right or left, depending on which way you have come, to cross the river via the bridge, thus following the direction for Mitsukama Falls and Mt. Mitake Climbing Path (三ツ釜の滝 御岳山登山口), and take the bitumen road uphill.

Ignore the small road to the right soon after, and proceed over the large water pipe (beneath the road). When the road divides about 6 minutes from the river, keep to the left, that is, the lower road, which is signposted for Ōnara Pass and Mt. Mitake (大栖峠を 圣て 御岳山に至る). The first of a number of trout fishing and breeding pools can be seen below to the left. Cross straight through the intersection a minute later, toward Unazawa Valley

and Mt. Ōtake (海沢谷 大岳山). The slope that appears almost immediately on your right has a stunning concentration in spring of the
beautiful mauve-colored *katakuri* (dogtooth violet), which grows
underground for nine months of the year and blooms in early
April. Chestnut trees also grow here. To your left is a trout farm,
the various pools containing fish of progressively larger size, and a
water-testing plant. Summer purple-and-white *tamaajisai* (hydrangea) and tiny blue *tsuyukusa* (dayflower or spiderwort) can be
found along the road edges.

About 5 minutes later, the road splits at Itsuke Bridge (*Itsuke-
bashi*, いつけばし). The main road to the left, which crosses the
river, leads up to Okutama Cemetery. Numerous purple spring
wildflowers, such as the tall *ōaraseitō* (*Orychophragmus violaceus*, a
violetlike plant), true violets, and corydalis decorate the edge of
this road in spring, and just before the cemetery's entrance gates a
path commences to Ōnara Pass, which is a later destination of this
walk. However, the route described here, via Mitsukama Falls, involves continuing straight on and thus avoiding crossing the
bridge, along the smaller road toward America Camp Village (アメ
リカキャンプ村). This road shadows the stream (on your left) and
boasts many more summer blossoms, including yellow brushes of
ōawadachisō (solidago goldenrod) and pink beads of *mama-
konoshirinugui* (polygonum), as well as the more common types.
The already-mentioned *tamaajisai*, whose expansive blossoms char-
acteristically begin as small ball-shaped buds, dominate the roadside edges all the way to the falls.

The remainder of the walk to the falls turnoff is relatively
straightforward. You will pass some houses, America Camp
Village (across the river, with camping huts, fire sites, etc.), and a
sawmill, and the now-gravel road begins to climb (via a number of
bridges and, in one instance, a tunnel) high above the river
through deep, photogenic ravines of the attractive Unazawa
Valley with its rapids and large boulders. Good shade is generally
offered by the native forest, but this has occasionally been supplanted by tree plantations. Beautiful yellow *matsuyoigusa* (oenothera evening primrose) and large blue butterflies can also be seen
along this section in summer.

At a bend in the road after about 45 minutes, you should reach the right-hand turnoff to Mitsukama Falls. A sign here (三ツ釜の滝 大岳山) indicates that this is also the way to Mt. Ōtake. Note that the latter part of the trail described resumes from this point.

Around Mitsukama Falls (35 minutes)

Beyond the wide entrance to the Mitsukama Falls (*Mitsukama-no-taki*, 三ツ釜の滝) area, which has a rest shelter and toilets, a trail continues via (in places rotting) wooden ladders and over rocky stream beds and small bridges through deciduous forest that in autumn provides a carpet of gold. Ignore the mountain path toward Mt. Ōtake (山道を圣て大岳山へ) after 5 minutes, and proceed straight on toward Mt. Ōtake via Mitsukama Falls, Nejire Waterfall, and Ō Waterfall (三ツ釜滝 ネジレ滝 大滝を圣て大岳山へ). You will have to climb metal stairs, and the path can be a little difficult to follow over the rocks. When after a couple of minutes you reach the stairs to the right, signposted for Mt. Ōtake (大岳山), you are at the lowest level of the falls (Mitsukama means "three cauldrons"). Anywhere here, or higher, would make a lovely lunch stop, as the sight of the gushing water is particularly appealing.

Climb the stairs to reach the falls' second level, with further falls above. A sign here indicates this is the continuation of Unazawa Valley and the direction of Mt. Ōtake (海沢谷 大岳山). Take the unmarked track that veers left down toward the stream after about 4 minutes. (The main trail makes its way up, sometimes through plantation and leaving the stream, toward Mt. Ōtake.) Descend the steel steps and follow the little-used path along the right bank of the stream, toward Nejire Waterfall (ネジレの滝 5分). This forest has white Japanese hydrangea and pink-and-white lily flowers in summer. In about 5 minutes you will reach Nejire Waterfall (*Nejire-no-taki*), a stunning grottolike hollow where water cascades from above.

Return to the road via the same path in reverse.

From Mitsukama Falls to Hatonosu Station (1 hour 40 minutes)

At the road, go right and uphill in the signposted direction of Ōnara Pass and Mt. Mitake (大栖峠を圣て 御岳山). There are some views of the valley to the left below, and hydrangeas, purple *hotarubukuro* (bellflower), and white *okatoranoo* (chlethra loosestrife)

Valley and mountain panorama from the road to Ōnara Pass.

wildflowers proliferate in summer. You may even see a few tiny pink sheaths of *komatsunagi* (indigo plant) at this time of year.

This old forest road is a very pleasant trail, and the extensive mountain views to the left increase with altitude. The surrounding forest consists mostly of plantations, but strips of native growth bordering the road add interest. Flowering shrubs, the occasional *kibushi* (*Stachyurus praecox*), yellow *fuki* (butterburr) in spring, and even some summer raspberries dot these narrow strips. The path narrows at one point where a landslide has occurred.

Ōnara Pass (*Ōnara-tōge*, 大栖峠) is reached in about 35 minutes, and is appropriately named (Ōnara means literally "big oak"). Under the shade of some huge old trees frequented by woodpeckers, you are faced with a choice of paths. The pleasant uphill track to the right (as you approach the pass) leads to Mt. Mitake (御岳山方面) (a walk to which is described in *Day Walks Near Tokyo*), while that along the ridge to your left is a pleasant though ultimately steep downward trail through lovely native forest toward Hikawa (林道圣て氷川方面) and, eventually, Mt. Shiro (城山),

and connects to the path from Okutama Cemetery. The route described here, however, is the wide, downhill path straight ahead, toward Hatonosu (鳩ノ巣方面).

Log-and-earth steps assist your descent in the early part, and more summer wildflowers, among them pink-white *amagiamacha* (Japanese hydrangea) and mauvish *ōbajanohige* (ophiopogon lily), flourish here. The trail is generally downhill and you will skirt farmhouses and various other buildings. Tracks, some marked, some not, lead off to destinations on the left and right, including several to Buttress Camp (バットレスキャンプ場) (a probable reference to nearby Shiroyama Dam), and you will pass some graves, but stay on the main track toward Hatonosu Station (鳩ノ巣駅). A delicate but attractive late spring/early summer trailside adornment is the white masses of tiny *yukinoshita* (saxifraga strawberry geranium).

After about 45 minutes, a trail slants back to the right toward distant Mt. Konpira (金比羅山に至る) and a few minutes later another descends toward Kori Station (an alternative, but farther, finishing point for this walk) via Sun-niwa and Kori-tsuki (寸庭 古里 附を圣て古里駅へ), but again continue on, toward Hatonosu Station via Sakashita Hamlet (坂下部落を圣て鳩乃巣駅) and Hatonosu (鳩の巣へ), respectively. This way leads you past cabins and kiosks and eventually becomes a bitumen road, which is joined by another road from the right and a footpath from the left.

After approximately 10 minutes, the road crosses the Tama River and winds its way up to the main thoroughfare about a minute away. There, turn left and then right up the road (with an adjacent mapboard and just before a tunnel) a minute or two on. The station is now just a few minutes away. Take the right-hand alternative where the road splits, and then the right-hand alternative again just before the railway line. You will need to cross to the far side of the platform to catch a train going in the correct direction.

To return to Shinjuku Station, take a train to Tachikawa, changing if necessary at Haijima (拝島) on the Ōme Line. At Tachikawa, change to the Chūō Line to Shinjuku. The fare for the entire journey is ¥1,030. (If you purchased an *Okutama-Akikawa jiyūkippu*, use this for the return trip.)

OKUMUSASHI

25. OKUMUSASHI NATURE TRAIL —— E

Course: Higashi-Moro Station (by taxi) → Lake Kamakita →
Kitamuki Jizō → Yaseone Pass → Mt. Monomi →
Mt. Takasashi → Mt. Hiwada → Koma Station

Reference map: Nitchi Map No. 20 (Okumusashi, 奥武蔵), Old
Series No. 1; or Shōbunsha Map No. 25 (Okumusashi Chichibu,
奥武蔵 秩父), Old Series No. 25.

Walking time: About 2 hours 30 minutes.

Points of interest: Scenic Lake Kamakita, good views of the
Kantō Plain and Okutama range, historical Koma Town.

GETTING THERE

At Ikebukuro Station, board a Tōbu Tōjō Line (東武東上線) limited
express (*tokkyū*, 特急) or one of the frequent expresses (*kyūkō*, 急行)
bound for Shinrin-kōen (森林公園) or Ogawa-machi (小川町). These
depart from Platform 1. Get off at Sakado (坂戸) Station (42
minutes by limited express, 45 minutes by express), and transfer
to the Ogose branch line (Platform 2/3) for the 15-minute ride to
Higashi-Moro (東毛呂). A single ¥580 ticket covers both legs of the
journey.

As the bus to *Kamakita-ko* (Lake Kamakita, 鎌北湖), no longer
operates, take a taxi from Higashi-Moro Station to the edge of the
lake. The three-kilometer journey will cost about ¥330 per person
for a group of four.

From Lake Kamakita to Kitamuki Jizō (45 minutes)

Lake Kamakita is well known for its *sakura* (cherry) trees (many
people visit it in April to view them), and for its colorful autumn
foliage. This man-made but pretty body of water is home to ducks
and a fleet of rowboats for hire, and the benches on its shores
make for relaxed sightseeing.

Near the top of the earthen dam wall that holds back Lake Kamakita's waters stands a vertical signpost. To begin the walk, you should head in the direction labeled for Kitamuki Jizō and Shukuya Waterfall (北向地蔵 宿谷ノ滝), that is, along the bitumen road which winds around the left-hand side of the lake. Perhaps 3 minutes along this road, past a car park, is Kamakita-ko Youth Hostel (鎌北湖ユースホステル). Veer left up the gravel path just before the youth hostel building.

This path, known as the Okumusashi Nature Trail (*Okumusashi shizen hodō*, 奥武蔵自然歩道), is signposted for Kitamuki Jizō and Musashi-yokote Station (北向地蔵 1.3 KM 武蔵横手駅 5.3 KM). The initially wide gravel path climbs, in places steeply, in the direction of Mt. Monomi (北向地蔵を至て物見山) through mostly plantation with a number of birds. Ferns grow on the sides of the path, and the ubiquitous *aoki* (laurel) and *tsubaki* (camellia) trees yield bright red berries and beautiful pink-and-yellow blossoms, respectively, in the first months of the year.

In some 15 minutes you will reach a major intersection with a concrete sign marker. Turn right here, toward Kinchakuda and Kitamuki Jizō (巾着田 北向地蔵を至て). Within 50 meters, the track, still marked as the Okumusashi Nature Trail, crosses directly over a surfaced road. On the other side, it climbs again, past *susuki* (pampas grass) on the left and cultivated fields and good views of Moroyama Town to the northeast (right). Avoid the lesser tracks off to the right.

Various indications on the trailside show how many trees, including *momi* (fir), *kashi* (oak), and *tsuga* (Japanese hemlock), have been regularly planted. Traditionally, the trees were cut down every 15–25 years for the production of charcoal, although this is becoming rarer. Other trees fringing the pleasant, wide trail here are *konara* (beech), *nurude* (sumac), and *shirakashi* (another kind of beech), mostly on the right.

The trail levels off, and in 10–15 minutes you arrive at a signposted fork, just before a surfaced road from which there are reasonable views of the Okutama range to the west (ahead). Between the fork and the road lies Kitamuki Jizō (the "northward-looking" guardian deity of travelers and children) within a tiny shelter. A makeshift bell hangs nearby.

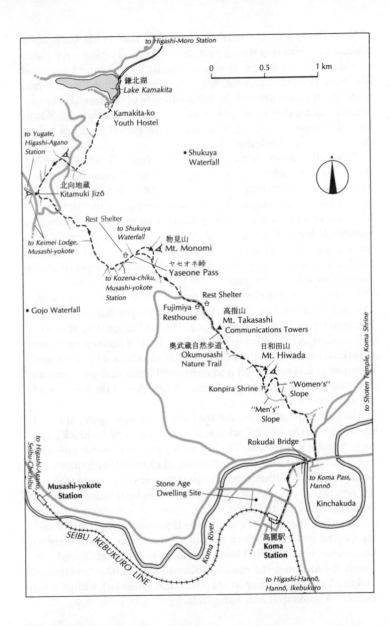

to Higashi-Moro Station

0   0.5   1 km

鎌北湖
Lake Kamakita

Kamakita-ko
Youth Hostel

Shukuya
Waterfall

N

to Yugate,
Higashi-Agano
Station

北向地蔵
Kitamuki Jizō

Rest Shelter

to Shukuya
Waterfall

物見山
Mt. Monomi

to Keimei Lodge,
Musashi-yokote

ヤセオネ峠
Yaseone Pass

to Kozena-chiku,
Musashi-yokote
Station

Rest Shelter

Gojo Waterfall

Fujimiya
Resthouse

高指山
Mt. Takasashi
Communications Towers

奥武蔵自然歩道
Okumusashi
Nature Trail

日和田山
Mt. Hiwada

Konpira Shrine

"Women's"
Slope

to Shoten Temple, Koma Shrine

"Men's"
Slope

Rokudai Bridge

to Higashi-Agano,
Seibu-Chichibu

Musashi-yokote
Station

Stone Age
Dwelling Site

to Koma Pass,
Hannō

Kinchakuda

高麗駅
Koma Station

SEIBU IKEBUKURO LINE

Koma River

to Higashi-Hannō,
Hannō, Ikebukuro

From Kitamuki Jizō to Mt. Hiwada (1 hour)

To the left across the road is a trail to Keimei Lodge and, eventually, Musashi-yokote (啓明荘 武蔵横手), which has a station on the Seibu Ikebukuro Line (西武池袋線). This would take about 50 minutes to complete. The path to the right also across the road leads on to Yugate and Higashi-Agano Station (ユガテ 東吾野駅) on the same line, about a 1 hour-25-minute walk whose final stretch is along a road. However, the trail described here involves *not* crossing the road, but simply veering left along the dirt path in the direction indicated on the concrete marker as being that of Kinchakuda via Mt. Monomi (巾着田 物見山を圣て).

The path descends past *noriutsugi* (a deutzialike hydrangea) and *hisakaki* (*Eurya japonica*, a kind of camellia) trees to a continuation of the road after approximately 7 minutes. Cross directly over the road, in the direction marked "Mt. Hiwada 3.1 km and Kinchakuda 5.3 km" (日和田山 3.1 KM 巾着田 5.3 KM), and continue straight uphill through the cutting.

Ignore the very large but unmarked path downhill to the right soon after. Similarly ignore other diverging paths, including two that branch off at the same point, one of which is labeled "Kozena-chiku and Musashi-yokote Station" (小瀬名地区 武蔵横手駅), to the right some 15 minutes later. After a level section through plantation, the way is a little up and down, and passes a rest shelter. At Yaseone Pass (*Yaseone-tōge*, ヤセオネ峠), about 7 minutes beyond the latter, labeled intersection, the path to Shukuya Waterfall (*Shukuya-no-taki*, 宿谷ノ滝) descends to the left. Some meters on, a track veers off to the left, up Mt. Monomi (*Monomi-yama*, 物見山). You can go either way, but this 375-meter peak has rest benches, excellent views, and is surrounded by fine native forest.

The path from the summit continues down the other side to rejoin the main trail. Proceed straight, in the direction of Mt. Hiwada and Kinchakuda (日和田山 巾着田), passing at one point a tiny shrine. Within 10 minutes, your path should merge with a road, near some fields. Follow this road for less than 10 minutes, past a rest shelter on the left and Fujimiya Rest House (a restaurant with a viewing platform popular for its Mt. Fuji panoramas), and an old thatched farmhouse on the right, to the

Looking back on the climb to Kitamuki Jizō.

communication towers on top of Mt. Takasashi (高指山). The marked trail to Mt. Hiwada (*Hiwada-san*, 日和田山) resumes downhill to the right.

As before, a number of lesser trails branch off, but continue for 10–15 minutes to where a steep, unmarked rocky path leads up to the left to the summit of Mt. Hiwada. Again, you can take either track, but as this peak offers a rest bench, an Edo-period Buddhist stela, some chimes, and excellent views of the Kantō Plain and the mountains, you may wish to make the climb.

From Mt. Hiwada to Koma Station (45 minutes)

The path from the summit descends steeply to reconnect with the main trail in the direction of Mt. Tenran via Kinchakuda (巾着田を経て天覧山). In about 5 minutes, you will reach Konpira Shrine, a small wooden building with an information board nearby. The shrine itself is not of great interest, but the view of Kinchakuda from the silver-colored *torii* (shrine gateway) on the rocky outcrop a little below is notable. As related on the information board, the name Kinchakuda (literally, "bag-shaped field") refers to the horseshoe or bag-shaped area of fields resulting from a sweeping bend in the Koma River visible below. Some of the large number of people who fled Korea more than twelve hundred years ago to settle in the district cultivated this Kinchakuda area, using the river for irrigation.

There are two paths leading down, although they rejoin later: a "women's" trail, and a "men's" trail. You are recommended to take the *onnazaka* (women's slope), marked 女坂 巾着田, since this is in better condition. Within 10 minutes, the men's path merges and you pass under a large concrete *torii*. About 5 minutes later, near a green wire fence, an unmarked track that could be taken as a shortcut to historical Koma Shrine (*Koma jinja*, 高麗神社) leads off to the left, but keep on the main path. The trail subsequently winds down for a few minutes to a bitumen road next to a water pumping station, where you should turn right, that is, in the direction of Koma's Stone Age Dwelling Site (高麗石器時代住居跡). From here to Koma Station on the Seibu Ikebukuro Line is only about 20 minutes.

Follow the road the short distance to where it meets another from the left. Go right, toward Koma Station (高麗駅) and the Stone Age Dwelling Site (石器時代住居跡), which is also the direction of Kinchakuda (きんちゃく田). (The road to the left leads to Koma Shrine and Shoten Temple [聖天院].) Ignore the small lane to the right marked "Koma Station" (高麗駅), and continue straight down to the main road and turn right. (If you bear left down the lane off this main road after 50 meters, and subsequently go right and then left across Kinchakuda's fields, you can walk on via Koma Pass [*Koma-tōge*, 高麗峠] to Higashi-Hannō Station [東飯能駅] on the JR Hachikō Line [JR八高線] or to Hannō [飯能], a main junction station on the Seibu Ikebukuro Line. This would take about 90 minutes.) To complete the walk to Koma Station described here, continue along the main road and cross the Rokudai Bridge (*Rokudai-bashi*, 鹿台橋) over the Koma River.

About 100 meters farther at a set of traffic lights, veer left and walk uphill to another set of lights. If you don't wish to visit the historically important but somewhat unspectacular site of a Jōmon (8,000–300 B.C.) stone age dwelling, continue straight through the lights and then cross the railway tracks by using the pedestrian path. On the other side, turn right and follow the small lane around to the station.

If you do want to look at the stone age site, turn right at the traffic lights, pass through a junction, also with signals, and then turn left up the signposted path about 100 meters beyond. The small roped-off site has a board that tells of the discovery here earlier this century of stone utensils, including plates, and axes. The positions of fireplaces and pillars are easy to see on the site. To reach the station, return to the junction with traffic lights and turn right. Pass under the railway line—the station is then on your left.

In front of the station are some totem poles, similar to those erected previously by the immigrant Koreans to ward off misfortune in their villages. The town's name, Koma, is actually another reading of the Chinese characters for Kōrai, the ancient Korean kingdom.

To return to Ikebukuro, catch a rapid express (*kaisoku kyūkō*, 快速急行). Alternatively, board a local train and transfer two stations down the line at Hannō Station to an express (*kyūkō*, 急行) to Ikebukuro. In either case, the fare is ¥460 and the train leaves from Platform 2 of Koma Station.

APPENDIX

The suggestions for Part A of this appendix are intended to provide readers with possibilities for year-round walking, taking into account not only the seasonal attractions of the area but also such factors as heavy snow in alpine regions and the cessation of bus services. Obviously, most walks will be at their most pleasant in spring and autumn (the two best times from the point of view of both scenery and weather).

Selecting walks for Part B was difficult because walks with outstanding attractions number many more than five. For this reason, visitors with limited time may wish to make their own list after reading the walk descriptions. The walks listed have been chosen to provide a representative slice of the Kantō District's appeal: a little history, ravine and waterfall scenery, mountain forest and lakeside trails, views of Mt. Fuji, and the chance of seeing Japanese animals.

A. Suggested walks according to season
SPRING
Old Yusaka Road (E)
Ōwaku Valley (M)
Lake Ashi (M)
Daibosatsu Pass (D)
The Ganman Pools (D)
Ō Mountain (D)
Mitsukama Falls (M)

SUMMER

Old Tōkai Highway (E)

Narusawa Ice Cave (E)

The Five Hundred Arhats (E)

Kirifuri Highland (M or E)

Lake Chūzenji (M)

The Twin Lakes of Kirikomi and Karikomi (M)

Mt. Wagakuni (D)

AUTUMN

Descending Mt. Fuji (M)

The Three Passes (D)

Mt. Shakushi (D)

Nishizawa Gorge (M)

Mt. Ontake (D)

Ume-ga-se Gorge (M)

Southern Takao Ridge (M or D)

WINTER

Bōsō's Ancient Mounds (E)

Kame-yama to Kiyosumi (M)

Kenchō Temple (E)

Okumusashi Nature Trail (E)

B. Five walks for the visitor with limited time

Old Yusaka Road (E)

Narusawa Ice Cave (E)

Nishizawa Gorge (M)

The Twin Lakes of Kirikomi and Karikomi (M)

Kame-yama to Kiyosumi (M)

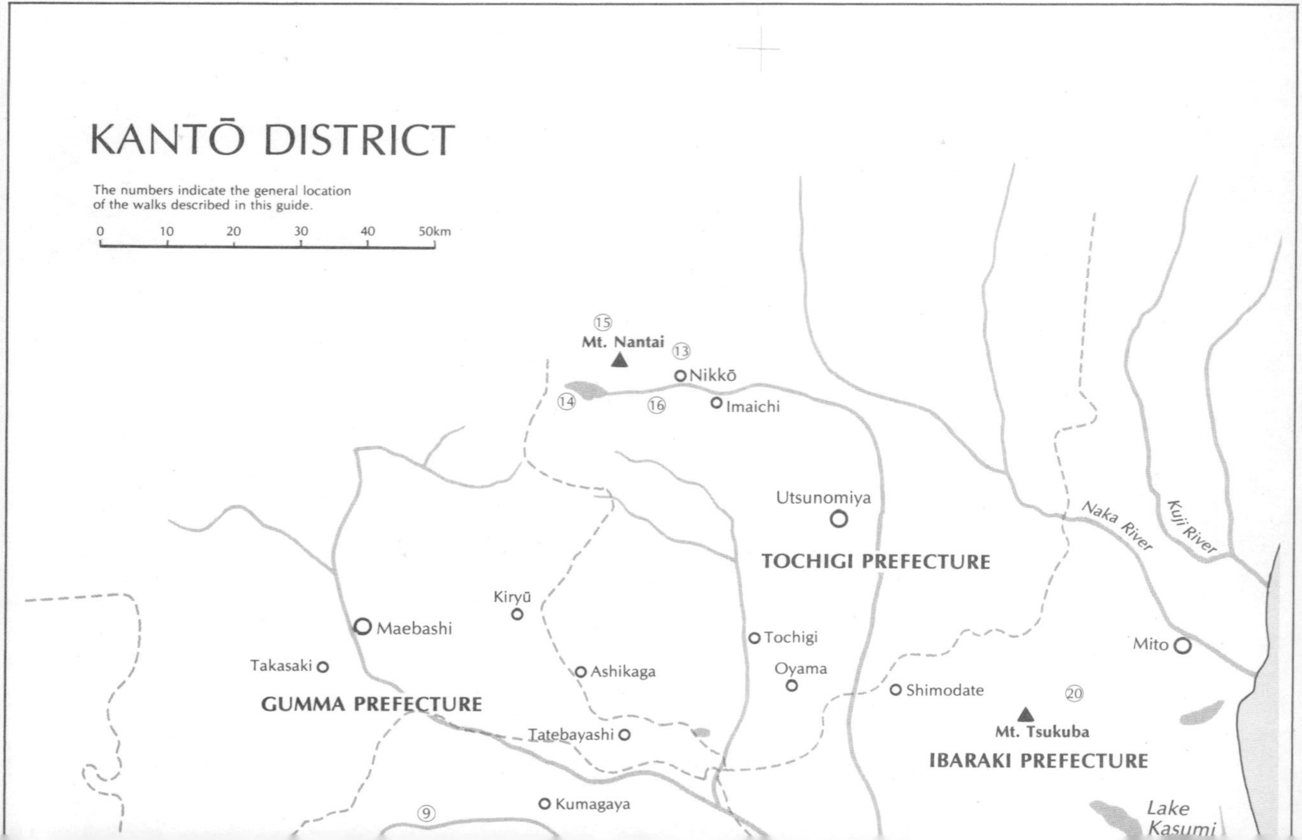

KANTŌ DISTRICT

The numbers indicate the general location of the walks described in this guide.

0 10 20 30 40 50km

GUMMA PREFECTURE

Takasaki ○

○ Maebashi

Kiryū ○

Ashikaga ○

Tatebayashi ○

○ Kumagaya

⑨

TOCHIGI PREFECTURE

⑮ Mt. Nantai ▲

⑭

⑯ ○ Imaichi

⑬ ○ Nikkō

○ Utsunomiya

Tochigi ○

Oyama ○

Shimodate ○

⑳ Mt. Tsukuba ▲

IBARAKI PREFECTURE

Mito ○

Lake Kasumi

Kuji River

Naka River